T0163595

it matters

it
matters
Looking for the Good Things in Life

amy lynne

NASHVILLE

NEW YORK • MELBOURNE • VANCOUVER

it matters
Looking for the Good Things in Life

Published in New York, New York, by Morgan James Publishing. Morgan James is a trademark of Morgan James, LLC. www.MorganJamesPublishing.com

The Morgan James Speakers Group can bring authors to your live event. For more information or to book an event visit The Morgan James Speakers Group at www.TheMorganJamesSpeakersGroup.com.

Scripture taken from the New American Standard Bible Copyright ©1960, 1962, 1963, 1968, 1971, 1972, 1973, 1975, 1977 by The Lockman Foundation, Used by permission.

ISBN 978-1-68350-599-0 paperback
ISBN 978-1-68350-600-3 eBook
Library of Congress Control Number: 2017907934

Cover Design by:
Rachel Lopez
www.r2cdesign.com

Interior Design by:
Bonnie Bushman
The Whole Caboodle Graphic Design

In an effort to support local communities, raise awareness and funds, Morgan James Publishing donates a percentage of all book sales for the life of each book to Habitat for Humanity Peninsula and Greater Williamsburg.

Get involved today! Visit
www.MorganJamesBuilds.com

I dedicate this book to my Dad and Mom.
Thanks for all the great adventures, and thanks
for teaching us how to love well.
I love you!

Contents

Foreword

There is no shortage of painful stories in life. If you have lived long enough, you too may have your own story. Most of us do. We don't plan for the pain. We don't readily embrace the hardships. Oftentimes, these just happen. They seem to come out of nowhere. In truth, they often come from poor choices we make or poor choices others make that affect us. This is the stuff of life isn't it? Unplanned. Unwanted. Unwelcome events that throw off our equilibrium or upend our plans. It is easy to become unhinged or unbalanced and wonder if God cares.

Amy's story is a lot like yours and mine. And Amy's story is unique too. She will not deny that she made a series of not-so-good choices. I have been there too and I am betting that you have as well. If you are someone who believes God loves you, He can also redeem these painful choices and remold you as a potter does with his clay. Amy allowed that remolding to occur. This doesn't mean the consequences of our bad choices magically disappear. But here's what it does mean. It means that God takes our painful choices and finds a way to remold our lives based on what is, not on what we think it should have been. That's the essence of the Christian life—transformation. We become a new creation.

This book is about real life and about Amy's experiences, but it is far more than that. It is also about how she allowed God to start over with her at times. God will always use what we give Him to work with. You can look at any biblical character and see they were imperfect human beings who God molded to accomplish great things. The seemingly small and large events that occur, often daily, do indeed matter. How easy it is for us to forget that our character is forged in the countless small choices that come at us daily, weekly, and yearly. How we respond to these determines the kind of people we will be. Indeed, character is simply an accumulation of the many choices we make through life—yes, they matter!

The good news is that even in the unexpected circumstances of life, the adventures, the pain, the disappointment, the failure—God is there for us. He is there waiting and willing to run toward us as He did with the prodigal son. In this sense, Amy's story is your story. Read it and be encouraged. Read it and see your failure as a stepping stone to God's grace. Read it and recognize that no matter what you have been through in life, God cares.

Don S. Otis

Introduction

Some years back, God placed the name of this book on my heart. It took me a while to dig deep to start writing it, but finally, I began. The words began to flow in my mind while on a road trip to the Great Smoky Mountains of Tennessee. On the five-hour drive, God filled my heart with the stories that would grace these pages—stories about life and the great adventures we experience each day.

During your journey through this book, you will read about life events and see how they help us understand how we need other people, how important our daily choices are, and how it matters that we have a relationship with God. These stories focus on the realities of life—some funny, some sad, some in between. In each story, I hope you can find God's grace and redemption and see how the story can provide a life lesson.

In our society, there is so much negativity and so many people focused on that negativity, which tends to breed a lot of stinkin' thinkin'. God doesn't like that very much—my opinion anyway. This book focuses on the positive side of life. It helps us see things that we so often take for granted. It helps us be mindful of the things that do matter. Have you thought lately about the following questions: 1) What matters to God? 2) What matters to you? 3) What matters? Does anything really matter anymore?

Get in a comfy spot with a cup of your favorite beverage, some soft pillows, your Bible, and relax as you read these stories. I hope most of them make you smile. At the end of each chapter, I'll share **Positive Word Confessions**, then I'll give you an **In the Word** Bible study, and at the very end, **Prayer Time**. When you finish reading this book, I hope your daily mental load will be a lot less burdensome and that your outlook will be more positive and hopeful. I hope you will be able to look back on this book, as well forward in your own life, and say, "It Matters!"

Positive Word Confessions. Please read these Scriptures out loud. I have added words in parentheses to make the verses personal to you. Personalizing God's Word helps it come alive in your heart.

In the Word. This will be a time of Bible study in relation to the stories you previously read.

Prayer Time. Please feel free to pray your own prayer, but you are welcome to pray with me and use my prayer. Please pray aloud. If using this in a group study, ask everyone to pray together and aloud.

it matters ...
In the Mountains

From the time I was a child, my family had great adventures in the Great Smoky Mountains of Tennessee. We visited there many times and in different seasons. I'm from Alabama, where we have mini-mountains, so seeing the Smokies was always a treat. As we would reach the top of the hill of a road and God's magnificent creation stared back at us, we'd say with utter joy and awe, "We've arrived!"

A two-lane road winds through the mountains and is surrounded by beautiful hardwood trees, rock precipices, and an occasional stop off for a walking trail. The road follows a constantly flowing creek. Today, I love to stop along the way, walk down the steep edge of the road to the creek bank, and sit and listen to the water bubbling and flowing over the smooth stones and think about the trout just waiting to be caught—yes, I'm a fisher woman. And when I was a child, you could always find us, no matter the time of year, taking off our shoes and walking out over the stones to feel the water rushing over our feet. Did you know wearing cotton socks will keep you from falling when you step on a slippery wet rock? Now you know!

In the mountains, we were always on the lookout for our next great adventure. In winter, the mountains would be covered with snow, which always lends itself to plenty of fun. Of course, Dad was always prepared for anything and everything. He would attach the snow chains to the tires of the vehicle, then tie a tow rope to the car bumper. Then we'd take turns being pulled on the sled.

Never a dull moment in our family!

We had many snowball fights and contests to see who could find the largest icicle on the side of the mountain. We hiked some of the trails only to get to the top and not see anything because, we were on the Great SMOKY Mountains.

There on the slopes at Ober Gatlinburg, I learned how to ski. I also tried ice skating, but that's not my thing. People with no balance and weak ankles aren't good ice skaters. Gatlinburg features beautiful waterfalls and nature trails, horseback riding, snow skiing, snow tubing, ice skating, zip-lines, mountain rails, and a gazillion gift shops. Oh, let's not forget the homemade candy stores in downtown Gatlinburg. You can't pass by without going into one to sample the many kinds of fudge and confections or get some taffy or some caramel popcorn. Okay, I'll stop now—I need some chocolate!

It matters that our family enjoyed spending time together.

While in my early twenties, three girlfriends and I visited the Smokies for a weekend of fun and hiking. We ate breakfast at the Pancake Pantry—my favorite place in the world for breakfast. Afterward, we headed up into the mountains to hike a six-mile trail. As we were driving up, it began to snow. We arrived at our destination and decided we'd probably only see a few snow flurries. We didn't have the weather online back then, but in retrospect, we should have watched the early morning weather report before heading out for the day. Anyway, we got out of our car and headed out on the trail.

The longer we hiked, the deeper the snow got. The trail led us to a narrow area on the side of a cliff with a rope attached. We had about two feet of walking space and were walking on six inches of snow with a steep drop sure to kill anyone who fell. All danger aside, we were determined to reach the top of that mountain, so we kept pressing forward.

After we reached the four-mile mark, we rested. That's when a group of hikers came down from the mountain and advised us not to go any farther because the path was beginning to ice over. The bunch of wimps that we were, we turned around and headed back to the car. After slipping and sliding on the way back down the trail, we reached the car to find it parked in six inches of snow. We tried backing out—no go. We decided that two of us would hike down the road to find help in the town that was at least ten miles away, while the other two would stay with the car. I was on the walking team that would head down the mountain to buy snow chains. I was not looking forward to climbing back to the car after we got the chains.

As we began walking, we were trying to figure out exactly how we were going to accomplish our task when, suddenly, a car with snow chains came zipping by. Thank God the guys in the car stopped, backed up, and asked if we needed a ride. We explained our predicament, so the two cute guys offered to take us into Gatlinburg, so we could buy some snow chains and get back to our friends. They seemed very nice. We discovered that they lived in another city not too far away from Gatlinburg and had been in the mountains enjoying the snow. Anyway, we got into town and paid an exorbitant amount of money for a set of chains, then we headed back up the mountain.

As we began our ascent, we were stopped by the closed gates across the road, which were monitored by a mountain patrol. The roads had been deemed impassable. We explained to the guard that our friends were stranded and needed help. We begged him to let us go back up the mountain. He opened the gates and allowed us through. We arrived back at our friends' car and they were thrilled to see us! The guys put the snow chains on our tires and followed us down the mountain to safety. We bought them dinner for all their troubles. That day, they were our angels.

It matters that we went back to rescue our friends.

It matters that we extended a kindness
to the two cute guys who helped us.

Several years ago, I spent the weekend in a friend's three-story log cabin in the Smokies. I wasn't alone. My then husband (he is my ex now and aka the other person) was on the trip, but I won't say too much about him. Anyway, the cabin was beautiful. Outside the main level, a walk-around deck with several swings, rocking chairs, and a hot tub comprised the scene. From any spot on the deck, we had a phenomenal view of the mountains. As you entered the front door, the kitchen was to the left and off of the kitchen was a bedroom and bath. To the right was an eating area, which opened into a great room with a couple of comfortable couches, a recliner, and a fireplace. Stairs led up from the great room into the loft. It contained a pool table surrounded by windows from which you could see a hundred miles of mountains. Breathtaking! The loft featured another bedroom and bath.

Back in the kitchen, a door led downstairs to the game room and to another bed and bath. Also on the ground level, you could go out a door onto a patio where the firewood was stored. A double-rail wood fence surrounded the patio, and a swing sat near the grill. The cabin also had little bears hanging from the rafters, the lights, and everywhere else—there were bear lights, a bear rug, bear plates, bear picture frames. You get the idea. The cabin was absolutely adorable.

The Smoky Mountains are known for black bear sightings. All that said, the other person and I decided to grill steaks for dinner and watch a football game. It was already dark outside, so we turned on the flood lights and walked down to the bottom level of the cabin and out onto the porch where we started the grill. As the steaks sizzled, we were on the swing talking about…

what else, but bears when he stopped suddenly. "I think I heard something," he said.

I laughed off his comment. A few minutes later, he walked upstairs to check on the potatoes cooking in the oven. I stayed behind to keep an eye on the steaks. As I sat on the swing without a care in the world, I heard something too. I turned my head to the left and through the double-rail fence, I saw the glare of the eyeball of a big black bear. Over the stack of firewood, I could also see the hump of his back. It's amazing to me everything you can see in the blink of an eye. The quickest route to the door lay between the swing and the fence. I think my blood-curdling scream stunned the bear. It gave me a chance to run by him and through the door. I couldn't have been more than a foot from him—just to give you a point of reference. Still screaming and on the other side of the door, I dead bolted it, ran through the other door, dead bolted it, and began my ascent up the stairs—screaming still. The other person opened the door at the top of the stairs as I flew through screaming, "THERE'S A BIG BLACK BEAR RIGHT DOWN THERE!" My words must have run together because he said, "What?" I said, still screaming, but slower this time, "THERE'S A BIG BLACK BEAR RIGHT DOWN THERE," as I pointed toward the bottom floor of the cabin. Guess what? He wanted to go see it.

We walked down the stairs, and as we opened the second of the two doors, we saw the bear. It appeared he wanted to join us for a steak dinner. The other person found a ten-foot pole just inside the door and pushed the bear away while I went and took the steaks off the grill. As soon as I got past the swing and headed for the door, the other person dropped the pole and ran into the cabin. We went out onto the deck of the second floor and watched the bear walk around for a while, then we went inside and ate dinner—without the bear.

At bedtime, I told the other person there was no way I could sleep in the loft. I reasoned that the bear could break into one of the doors, walk up the stairs, and eat us. The only way out of the loft was down the stairs, so we would have no way of escape. He asked, "Do you think the bear is Cujo or something?" I said, "Very funny. I have to be where I can run out one door if the bear bursts through the other one." He said, "What about me?" I just looked at him. It was his choice to camp out in the loft and get eaten—not mine. I was terrified and would not have been able to sleep. So I stayed on the second floor with the car keys in my pocket, built a happy little fire in the fireplace, reclined on the couch, and watched the fire for hours. About three that morning, the bear came up on the deck and walked around the cabin. I was terrified! The next morning, I called my friend who owned the cabin and told her about the bear encounter.

"Oh, I have always wanted to see a bear at my cabin," she said.

She had no sympathy for the terrified one—me.

It matters that I was terrified.

POSITIVE WORD CONFESSSIONS

(Read these verses out loud and make them personal to you. The verse says, "You will not . . ." Read it, "I will not . . .")

"You (I) will not be afraid of the terror by night, or of the arrow that flies by day; of the pestilence that stalks in darkness, or of the destruction that lays waste at noon." *Psalm 91:5-6*

(I will) "honor your (my) father and mother; and you (I) shall love your (my) neighbor as yourself (myself)." *Matthew 19:19*

IN THE WORD

Read Exodus 20:1-17, and write the first four commandments from verses 3-11 and the last six commandments from verses 12-17:

1.
2.
3.
4.
5.
6.
7.
8.
9.
10.

Read Mark 12:28-31, and write verses 30-31:

_____
_____
_____

_____

_____

In Exodus, the first four commandments are to love God; the last six commandments are to love our neighbor. Neighbor could be a family member, a friend, your next-door neighbor, or even a stranger. God is all about loving on you, and He is all about you loving on Him and others. What if you don't like someone? How is it possible to love someone you do not even like?

Read Romans 12:9-21, and write verse 14:

_____

_____

Bless and do not curse. That's a tough one! I first put this verse into practice when I prayed for someone who had abused me. When I say "abused," I mean to treat in an improper or wrong way. That can cover any number of things. My first attempt went something like this, and with gritted teeth, I might add: "Father, I pray spiritual blessings on _____." At that very moment, even though it was with gritted teeth, my words went into action. I put God's Word into practice and blessed this person, instead of cursing them. Why would you want to bless someone who has hurt you? Because God's Word says to do so, and that's good enough.

You can never understand God's ways or comprehend the thoughts of God or understand why He would want you to bless a person who has hurt you, but you can take God at His Word and you can have faith that He is big enough to take care of things for you. Like it says in Romans 12:19, "Never take your own revenge, beloved, but leave room for the wrath of God, for it is written, 'Vengeance is Mine, I will repay,' says the Lord."

Make a list of the people who have treated you in an improper or wrong way:

_____

_____

It will be very hard at first, and you may not want that person to be blessed financially or in any other way, so I would like to encourage you to pray spiritual blessings over each person. This way you are giving the person to God. You are speaking God's Word over them by blessing them, and you have the confident assurance in knowing that the wrath of God is in action. Yeah, that sounds a little vengeful, but God's Word says it in Romans 12:19, so it must be okay. Right?! That might make you feel a little better about praying blessings over someone who has hurt you. God's vengeance is redemptive. Our vengeance is usually hurtful. So try putting it into practice.

Please pray spiritual blessings over the people you previously listed, and do it one by one. Don't lump them all together.

Do this daily. You may not want to, but you will not believe the freedom you will experience by blessing someone who has hurt you.

PRAYER TIME

Holy Father, I love you so much! Thank you for helping me put into practice Your Word of praying for people who have hurt me. Thank you for releasing these hurts in my heart to You, and thank you for taking Your vengeance on these people who have hurt me. Please help me love You more every day. Please help me love my neighbors. I know not everyone is like me, and I need You to help me understand the differences in my neighbors and appreciate the unique way You designed each of us. "I will give thanks to Thee, for I am fearfully and wonderfully made; wonderful are Thy works, and my soul knows it very well" *(Ps. 139:14)*. Thank you for healing my heart of the wounds these people have inflicted through the years. I want to love You and love others the way You want me to love. Lord, I praise You and give You honor and glory and blessings. Great are You Lord and worthy to be praised! In the name of Jesus, Amen.

it matters ...
That You Walk in Forgiveness

F rom the time I was sixteen until I became a Christian at twenty-five, my life had been a nightmare. A lot of bad choices had led to some really bad consequences. I was five years into my Christian walk and had just finished reading Psalm 51 about David asking God to cleanse his heart from the sin in his life. I believed that God also wanted my heart cleansed from the sin in my life, so I prayed and asked God to cleanse my heart. God hears our prayers and is faithful to answer them, according to His will. "And this is the confidence which we have before Him, that, if we ask anything according to His will, He hears us. And if we know that He hears us in whatever we ask, we know that we have the requests which we have asked from Him" *(1 John 5:14-15)*. I felt certain God wanted my heart to be clean from all the junk in my past, so that was a no-brainer prayer for me to ask God. Soon after I prayed this prayer, God took me on a year-long journey of seeking forgiveness from people I had wronged. This was also a time of forgiving those who had wronged me. The following stories are just a sampling of the forgiveness journey that year:

When I was twelve, my family was very involved in a youth football program. The adults had created a haunted house to raise money for the initiative. One day, I was waiting for Dad to finish setting up props and saw a roll of tickets lying near his tools—the kind of tickets that are rolled up and purchased at a carnival to get on a ride. I took fifteen of them. I figured I would save my allowance and get in for free while the haunted house was operational. After the fundraiser ended, Dad, and whoever else was involved, accused the ticket lady of stealing fifteen dollars. Who knew they would have kept count of the tickets sold? My twelve-year-old mind had not thought that far ahead. To this day, I do not know how Dad found out I took the tickets, but he did. You've heard the saying, "Spare the rod, spoil the child." I believe that comes from Proverbs 22:15. Let's just say I was not a spoiled child, and fifteen dollars was garnished from my allowance.

Eighteen years later, God put this event on my heart. He wanted me to locate the ticket lady and apologize to her, but eighteen years was a long time. I prayed and asked God to help me find her. It's amazing how faithful God is, because two weeks later she began working with the same company where I worked. Isn't that just like God?! I introduced myself and reminded her who my parents were. She remembered them and asked how they were doing. After that, for two weeks I pondered how I was going to ask her for forgiveness. This was a new concept for me. One day we were both in the copier room. I reminded her about the event from years ago, I apologized, and asked her to forgive me. "Amy," she said, "if you had never brought that up, I would have never remembered that happened."

She may not have remembered, but God did and He wanted that out of my heart.

It matters that I had stolen and
someone else was wrongly accused.

When I was sixteen, I took my cat to the vet for a procedure. The next morning when I arrived at the vet's office to take her home, she was not ready. They asked me to come back later. When I arrived again to pick up my cat, the lady asked me if I had paid that morning. I lied and told her yes. God brought that instance up in my heart, and I was thinking, *Really, God?!* He really did want me to have a cleansed heart. I looked up the animal clinic—they were still in business. So I wrote them a check for thirty dollars and included a letter explaining what the money was for and asked for their forgiveness for lying to them and stealing from them. I took my cashed check as their acceptance of my apology.

It matters that I stole from them and lied to them.

That same year, I had a summer job doing clerical work at an insurance agency downtown. I was driving to work in rush-hour traffic one morning when, suddenly, a woman plowed into the driver door of my car. I did not see her coming from the far lane. Luckily, we were driving slow and she was turning across three lanes of traffic, so neither of us sustained any injuries. Of course, we called the police to have a report filed. The woman told me she did not have any insurance and that her father did auto body work and could fix the dent in my car. I gave the information to Dad, who called the lady's father. He explained to Dad that he could indeed fix my car and asked him to bring it to his house. Dad and I drove across town to see him. When we pulled up, we spotted a beat-up old truck with little round holes all over it. The man approached us and pointed to this truck as an example of the "phenomenal job" he had performed repairing his own vehicle.

Dad said it looked like he had taken a plunger-type tool, screwed it into the dent, and popped it out. Then, Dad said, he'd done a really bad job patching it up and painting the damaged area. Dad had already decided he wasn't going to let the guy fix my car, but he wanted to hear what the man had to say. The man looked at my car and said, "I can fix that. Oh, that's just a butterfinger dent." Dad and I looked at each other with the same thought: *What's a butterfinger dent?* We never found out exactly what it was. We left, Dad did the repair work on my car, and we never looked back. We just had to forgive and forget. Anytime any of us had a wreck after that, we just said, *Oh, that's just a butterfinger dent.*

It matters that my car had a butterfinger dent.

POSITIVE WORD CONFESSIONS

"Create in me a clean heart, O God, and renew a steadfast spirit within me. Do not cast me away from Thy presence, and do not take Thy Holy Spirit from me. Restore to me the joy of Thy salvation, and sustain me with a willing spirit. Then I will teach transgressors Thy ways, and sinners will be converted to Thee." *Psalm 51:10-13*

"But if we (I) walk in the light as He Himself is in the light, we (I) have fellowship with one another (others), and the blood of Jesus His Son cleanses us (me) from all sin." *1 John 1:7*

IN THE WORD

Forgiveness is not just about what you have done to others, but it is also about what has been done to you. There is no sin that is bigger than another. Sin is sin to God. He does not categorize sin, but we seem to.

Please write Matthew 6:14-15:

_____

_____

_____

_____

You can't walk away from that one!

Please write Matthew 18:21-22:

_____

_____

_____

_____

Plenty of Scripture verses address forgiveness. The ones just mentioned were just a few good verses to share with you. You need forgiveness because of sin. Romans 3:23 says, "For all have sinned and fall short of the glory of God." Sometimes it is very hard to let go and forgive people who have hurt us.

The following activity helped me understand how to forgive: I put a person's name on a piece of paper. Next to the name I wrote what that person had done to hurt me. I had a cross hanging on my wall. I took that cross down and laid it on the piece of paper with the name on the left side of it and the hurts on the right side. The cross put everything into perspective for me. Jesus not only died on the cross to save me from my sins, he also died on the cross to save the person listed on the left side of the cross as well. Had I ever done anything to hurt someone else? Yes. I am a sinner too. The hurt listed on the right side of the cross was sin. Who is the author of sin? The devil.

Please write 1 Peter 5:8:

_____

_____

_____

What I realized that day is: 1) the devil uses others, sometimes those closest to you, to sin against you—to hurt you, and 2) the devil uses you to sin against/hurt, sometimes those closest to you.

So instead of being mad at the person listed on your piece of paper, be mad at the devil.

Using the cross below, please take a few minutes to make your own list of people who have hurt you and the sin/hurts they committed against you:

Once you have finished making your list, look at the cross and in your mind you will be able to label the people on the left side as sinners and the hurts on the right side as sin.

Please read Romans 3:23 again.

God has forgiven you. Can you forgive those who have hurt you?

PRAYER TIME

Holy Father, it's so hard to see the people who have hurt me in the same light as myself—a sinner. Lord, where would I be without Your grace, without Your forgiveness, without Jesus? Are these people who hurt me saved? I pray for the salvation of _____ (list the people on your paper). Lord, please forgive me of all my sins and help those people who I have sinned against, to forgive me. Help me to walk in a spirit of forgiveness. When someone offends me, hurts me, uses me, or talks ugly to me, I can realize it is the devil coming against me, therefore I can forgive that person, but be mad at the devil. I don't have to be best friends with them or invite them back into my life, but I can forgive. Thank you Lord for forgiving me and giving me freedom. In the name of Jesus, Amen.

it matters ...
Regarding the Choices You Make

Years ago, in a time before cell phones, I was driving to work on the interstate, minding my own business when, suddenly, I saw smoke coming out from the hood of my car. Immediately, I pulled over into the emergency lane. Upon opening my hood, I noticed a lack of water in the radiator. I do have a general knowledge of cars. Dad had made sure I could change a tire and change my oil. I have even assisted with putting on a pair of brake pads—I held the light while Dad did the brake job. Does that count? In any event, I knew enough about cars to know I was stranded. I began to hike to the nearest place with a phone, so I could call Dad. Of course, that day I was wearing a dress and heels. Into my twentieth or so step, a car pulled over. It was not just any car, but a beat-up Chevy Camaro. The driver was a male with dreadlocks. Please note—I'm not opposed to someone having dreadlocks, but in a beat-up Camaro on the side of an interstate, the total picture made me a little wary.

I stood trying to decide whether to make a run for it in the heels, lock myself in my car, or pray. I chose the latter of the three and prayed that God send immediate help. Suddenly, another car—a Buick Regal—pulled over. It came closer to me than the Camaro. The guy was clean-cut and appeared to be nice, but Ted Bundy had been too. He rolled down his window and asked if I needed a ride. I smiled, as I looked toward his backseat and saw about two hundred yellow rubber duckies. I thought, *How bad could he be?* I thanked him for stopping and climbed into the passenger side of his car. The first words out of my mouth were, "What's with all the little yellow rubber duckies?" Come to find out, he had been in charge of the rubber ducky race the past weekend at a local state park and was taking the ducks back to their home until the next race came along. This very nice man dropped me off at a nearby mall and waved goodbye. I called Dad.

It matters that I was helpless and needed a helping hand.

When I went into full-time ministry, I knew it would be unlike anything I had experienced. One reason why: I had to raise my own support. Anyone who knows me knows that I'm a giver. Givers have a hard time begging for money and accepting handouts. I was totally focused on the ministry work at hand and knew God well enough to know that He would provide for me and my daughter—I was a single mother. Though my fundraising efforts were greatly lacking, I did try my best. My financial resources were so depleted that I didn't know where our next meal would come from. It was a beautiful Sunday morning, and I had planned to stay home from church and use the gas money to buy what groceries I could afford. I prayed and asked God to provide food for us. God spoke to my heart. He wanted me to go to church. I always tried to listen and be obedient when the Lord spoke to me, so I got myself and my daughter ready and headed to His House.

We arrived at church and were just about to enter its doors when a friend came up to me and said, "Amy, you are probably going to think this is really weird, but God put this on my heart and I need to share it with you." I readily agreed to hear what she had to say. She explained, "My husband does not eat leftovers, so this week I started bagging them up and putting them in the freezer each night. This morning, God put on my heart to ask you if you would like to have our leftovers every week." WOW! She further elaborated, "I brought them this morning and put them in the freezer in the Fellowship Hall. Just go downstairs, and get them when you leave church today."

We ate her leftovers for a year! During this time, I decided I was not good at fundraising. I went back into the secular workforce, so I could receive a steady paycheck.

It matters that my daughter and I did not have any food to eat.

My employer gives us the opportunity to support different charities by allowing us to pay five dollars for the privilege of wearing jeans at work for a day. On a particular day that I wore jeans, I had slept late and my hair wasn't all that it could have been. I had been working for a while at my happy little desk job and had gotten up to run to the restroom. I had just washed and dried my hands and was about to exit, when a lady I had never seen walked in. She said, "Oh, am I glad to see you." I wasn't sure what to say, so I just stood there. She went on, "This bathroom has been a mess this morning, and I'm so glad you're here to clean it up. You don't know how important you are to us." I responded, *"No hablo Español."* I walked out. That evening, I told my daughter about it. She laughed and said, "You were supposed to say, *"No hablo Inglés."* Whatever works!

It matters that I was involved in a case of mistaken identity because I was having a bad hair day and had paid to be casual.

One summer, the other person and I were renovating our lake house. Our area had been experiencing a severe drought like none we had ever seen. It had been so hot and so dry that the five feet of water at the edge of our seawall had dried up and left a big mud patch. *With the water down*, I kept thinking, *I could get out there and pull up the weeds that have started to grow in the water*. I kept waiting, because I wanted the mud to be dry in order to have a more solid base to stand on.

After several weeks, I was ready to begin my fun-filled task of weed pulling, so I slipped on my flip-flops, put on my gardening gloves, and headed for the lake. I stepped off the seawall to find that area of the lake bed was firm. As I began pulling up the weeds, I slowly worked my way out from the seawall. The farther out I went, the mushier the ground became.

I soon found myself ankle deep in mud. No problem. I gathered all the weeds I could reach, threw them up on the bank, and continued to step farther out. This time, instead of the mud coming up to my ankles, it came up to my left knee. To keep from falling, my right leg joined the fun and became entrenched in the mud as well. I tried to get my legs out, but the more I moved, the deeper I sank. The muddy concoction I stood in was like quicksand. I stood there completely unable to move my legs. I was about two yards out from the seawall and couldn't even lean in far enough to reach it to pull myself out of the muddy mess.

I had to break down and call the other person. I called his name, and within a few minutes I saw him come around the corner of the house. I informed him I was stuck and couldn't move. When he arrived, he crossed his arms, smiled, and said, "I like this!" I rolled my eyes and asked him to help me. He extended his arm, I grabbed a hold of it, and he began to pull me from the mud. My flip-flops received a muddy burial that day and will never be seen again.

That night God took me to His Word in Psalm 40:1-3: "I waited patiently for the Lord; and He inclined to me, and heard my cry. He brought me up out of the pit of destruction, out of the miry clay; and He set my feet upon a rock making my footsteps firm. And He put a new song in my mouth, a song of praise to our God; many will see and fear, and will trust in the Lord." God revealed to me that when we get stuck in the miry clay of life and we attempt to break free on our own, we are unable to do so in our own strength. God showed me how much we need Jesus to be our Rock and how we need others to help us get out of the miry clay we find ourselves stuck in at different times in our lives.

It matters that we call out for help when
we're stuck in the miry clay of life.

After she had been divorced for a couple of years, my daughter started dating again and asked me to screen her dates. I thought that was a really good idea. We agreed that she would not bring any guys home that she met online. She and the guy could meet, get to know each other, and if they liked each other well enough to move forward, then the guy would need to come over for a meet and greet with Mama Bear.

Recently, my daughter had been talking with a guy who was a friend of a friend of a friend kind of thing, but she had met him online. She said he was very funny and interesting. She wanted me to meet him. We planned for him to arrive at my house after I had returned from taking the grandkids out for dinner and a little bit of shopping. The guy was thirty years old and had a job, but I knew nothing else about him.

As the kids and I pulled up in the driveway, I spotted what I figured was his car—a new Nissan Maxima. *Ding*: Red Flag #1. How many thirty-year-old guys drive a Nissan Maxima over a nice, cool, new muscle car? My opinion anyway. Also, I noticed there was no license plate on his car. *Ding*: Red Flag #2. The kids and I opened the door to the house and walked inside. The kids met the guy and then wandered off to play a game while we sat down to chat.

Usually, I had about twenty odd questions I would ask with two of the questions being: 1) Do you drink?, and 2) Do you use drugs? This day was no exception. He said he did not use drugs, but did have an occasional drink. I went on with the questioning and thought again about the fact that his car did not have a license plate. I mentioned to him that I thought his car was nice and asked him how long he had owned it. He said it had been about three months, "but I trade cars all the time." *Ding*: Red Flag #3. In Alabama, you have thirty days to transfer title on a car. Why does he trade cars all the time? Was he in major debt from all the depreciation?

Because this guy already had three Red Flags against him, I decided he would not be in line to become my future son-in-law, but I continued to be nice and respectful toward him, hoping he would soon leave. There was just something about him I did not like, but I couldn't quite put my finger on it. I was trying to make small talk, so I mentioned that one of my neighbors had brought a jar of apple pie moonshine to the potluck supper the night before and that I didn't know stuff like that was legal. I don't know why that thought popped into my head; maybe I was trying to test the guy because he said he didn't drink much. The guy responded, "Oh, that kind of moonshine is legal, but it tastes like water compared to what I make." *Ding*: Red Flag #4. I responded, "Oh, you make your own moonshine, do you?" He went on to tell me all about the different flavors of moonshine he made. The more he talked, the more I could envision an encampment of sheriff cars lined up around our house to take us all to jail, because he probably had illegal moonshine in the trunk of his car.

Finally, I said that the kids had to start getting ready for bed and I thanked him for answering my questions. I breathed a sigh of relief as I saw his car backing out of my driveway. After he was gone, my daughter asked me what I thought of him. We sat down on the couch. I asked her, "Do you know the time period for transferring title on a car and obtaining a license plate?" She responded, "It's thirty days." I affirmed. I informed her, "There was no license plate on his car, and he said he had owned it for three months." Then I asked her, "Did you know about him making moonshine?" She said, "We just now talked about it before he left, and Mom, he said he doesn't drink it, but he makes a lot of money selling it." *Ding*: Reg Flag #5. That explains the no license plate and constantly trading cars—he's running moonshine. He's out!

It matters that you date people who respect the law.

POSITIVE WORD CONFESSIONS

"But (I will) seek first His kingdom and His righteousness; and all these things shall be added to you (me)." *Matthew 6:33*

"(I will) Be anxious for nothing, but in everything by prayer and supplication with thanksgiving let your (my) requests be made known to God." *Philippians 4:6*

IN THE WORD

Take a look at Abraham. He and Sarah were old, and Sarah had been barren for years. God made a covenant with Abraham in Genesis 17, and God kept telling him how He would bless Abraham and his descendants. God explained that Sarah would have a child. What did Abraham do? He laughed. He's like, "Yeah, right God." Anyway, God eventually delivered on His promise to open Sarah's womb and blessed her with a child. Fast forward to Genesis 22. God instructed Abraham to go and offer his only son, Isaac, as a burnt offering. If it were my child I would've said, *Excuse me, what?* You do not read about any doubt nor wavering of faith, you only read about obedience.

Please read Genesis 22:1-19, and write verse 5:

_____

_____

_____

There was no doubt in Abraham's heart that "we will worship and return to you." Abraham fully trusted God, and no doubt Abraham remembered the covenant God had made with him back in Genesis 17. Abraham did not understand what

God was up to or why God told him to sacrifice his only son; he only knew that he needed to be obedient to the Lord. Abraham was confident that God would provide. As Abraham had his knife in hand ready to slay his beloved Isaac, an angel of the Lord stopped him. God saw that Abraham feared Him enough to give up his son, therefore, God provided a ram for the burnt offering. Abraham called that place "The Lord Will Provide."

God will provide for you too. God has probably already provided for you in ways that might seem impossible for the human mind to conceptualize.

Please list the times when you knew, without a shadow of a doubt, that God supernaturally provided for you:

_____

_____

_____

_____

Please read Mark 4:35-40, and answer the following questions:

Were the disciples afraid?

Where was Jesus?

What happened to the storm when they called on Jesus?

Do you see how God provided for the disciples in this stormy situation? The disciples were afraid, but was Jesus? No.

He was asleep in the boat during the storm. When the disciples woke Jesus and got Him involved, He calmed the storm. If you feel like the storms in life are more than you can handle, call on Jesus to calm them. Whether it be needing a ride with a guy who has a bunch of rubber duckies in his backseat or having a friend give you her leftovers for a year, He will make a way where there seems to be no way, and He will provide everything you need. "Trust in the Lord with all your heart, and do not lean on your own understanding. In all your ways acknowledge Him, and He will make your paths straight" *(Prov. 3:5-6)*.

God also provides a way to move on from hurtful events in your past. Have you ever thought about how storms in your life or negative events can leave behind negative emotions? Believe it or not, to have a positive outlook on life, sometimes you must look within to determine if you are carrying around any negative baggage from a past hurt or past relationship gone bad. I would like for you to see how these negative emotions trigger a variety of negative responses throughout your life, so that you can identify them and bring about a positive response instead.

Shame and Guilt. These two go hand in hand. Shame tends to keep you withdrawn from others, and guilt is the sense that you have done something wrong or something you regret. Both will put you in a withdrawal mindset.

For years, I lived with shame and guilt as my constant companions after I had an abortion at the age of eighteen. I made some very bad choices when I was a teenager and lived to regret them. I finally discovered that the longer I chose to live with these bad choices, I would never be free and I would never have peace. The day I opened the door to this sin in my life, I gave the devil a foothold to condemn me. I felt the shame and guilt almost every day, and I could not seem to break free of this stronghold. Often, I wished I could go back and change the past.

Beloved, I would like you to see how shame and guilt will eventually deaden your desires for any type of meaningful and trustworthy relationships. They make you feel as though you are not worthy to allow anyone into your life to care about you. All too many times, you can put on a happy face at church, at work, or with your family, but inside there is constant turmoil. The thought of sharing your life with another person is quickly squelched at the prospect of being rejected or condemned. You can work very hard at pretending everything is okay, but is there anyone who knows the real you? I would like to share a story in the Bible of a young lady who knew the feeling of shame and guilt all too well. Her name was Tamar.

Please read 2 Samuel 13:1-20. After doing so, please describe how Tamar lived the rest of her life:

_____

_____

She was a beautiful woman who remained desolate because she was abused. Can you relate to Tamar?

_____

_____

_____

_____

Please take a few minutes to look back and identify any events in your past that might have opened the door for shame and guilt to torment you:

_____

_____

_____

Take these events to the cross and give them to Jesus. Ask Jesus to bring healing in your heart.

Contempt. This is a disrespectful attitude toward yourself and others. When a person has experienced a great deal of hurt, they tend to allow contempt to thrive in their life. It's as if everything on the inside of your body is in turmoil, so everything on the outside has to be perfect. A contemptuous attitude makes you feel unworthy of being loved. It also makes you think that you do not fit in anywhere, no one wants you around, or that something is wrong with you.

When contempt permeates your life, your attitude is that of being critical toward not only yourself, but everyone around you. No one can live up to your expectations—not even yourself. You always strive for perfection, but are never satisfied with the results. You constantly stay busy to avoid any close interaction with other people.

Describe how you respond when someone pays you a compliment:

_____

_____

_____

_____

_____

I was one who could never receive a compliment. While I was dealing with all these negative emotions in my own life, I ran into a friend at a local store. She knew what I was going through. Being such a good friend, she tested me and said, "You look so beautiful today!" When I heard the word "beautiful," I thought, *That's not me. I'm not beautiful.* I just stood there and began to weep. I could not express any gratitude for the compliment due to the contemptuous attitude I had toward myself. I did not see myself as beautiful, therefore, I could not receive her compliment. My friend hugged me and said, "One day, you will be able to say 'Thank you,' and you will see yourself the way others see you—beautiful." Her words gave me a sense of hope, and my weeping turned to tears of gratitude. I now realize my inward beauty toward God, and I can appreciate who I am as a child of God.

I want to say to you today, "You are beautiful! Please see yourself the way God and others see you!" Look in the mirror every morning and say, "I am beautiful!"

Please write Proverbs 31:30:

_____

_____

_____

_____

_____

Bitterness. This emotion eats away at the core of your soul. It lies in wait in the remote parts of your heart to spew forth its nastiness on some unsuspecting victim.

You can present a happy face before the world to see, but behind the happy face, bitterness hides. Whenever you have the possibility of a close relationship with someone, the bitterness has a way of spilling out to destroy whatever type of bond was beginning to form. Most bitter people run away from close relationships.

Please read Exodus 15:22-26.

Moses had brought the Israelites out of Egypt on their way to the Promised Land. They had been traveling for days without water and finally came to the waters at Marah. Behold, water for their parched tongues! They drank from the water hoping to find refreshment, but instead they only found bitterness. Moses cried out to the Lord to help them. The Lord instructed him to throw a tree into the water; the water then became sweet and drinkable. The tree was an Old Testament picture of what was to come in the New Testament with the cross of Christ. When you apply the cross to the bitterness in your life, the bitter will become sweet.

Please write Hebrews 12:15:

_____
_____
_____
_____

You have the power to overcome the root of bitterness by the grace of God! Ask God today to show you the bitter areas in your life, so you can specifically ask for forgiveness or extend forgiveness in those areas. Do you want to be approachable? Do you want others to find refreshment in you, instead of bitterness? You have the power to ask for forgiveness and to forgive others.

Please list the bitter areas of your life. Look at them throughout the week. Ask God to release these hurts and get them out of your heart.

Anger. There are two types of anger: righteous and unrighteous.

Righteous—A righteous anger results in godly sorrow over sin. A righteous anger concerns itself with injustices done to others. For instance, when you discover a child has been sexually abused or when someone throws a baby in a dumpster.

Unrighteous—An unrighteous anger seeks its own desires. When someone does not comply with your wishes or desires, you get angry. For instance, when you are standing too long in a line at the supermarket or you don't get to watch your favorite TV show.

Please answer the following questions:

Do you want justice from those who have wronged you?

_____

_____

With whom are you angry?

_____

_____

_____

What do you want out of your anger?

_____

_____

_____

How is this anger benefiting you?

_____

_____

_____

Have you misunderstood the situation?

_____

_____

_____

What would Jesus do?

_____

_____

_____

When I first asked myself these questions, my answers were not very honorable. I hope you did better with your responses. Does the last question tug at your heart? Instead of taking vengeance into your own hands, turn it over to God. When you adopt an attitude of a righteous anger, this is what results: God will get the glory; there is hope, and it allows an open door for repentance.

Fear. Fear (Ealse Evidence Appearing Real) is the feeling of being out of control or perhaps in danger. Whenever you have been in an abusive situation, you probably experienced great fear. Unfortunately, you may have never felt like you were rescued from that danger. Now, you have the strength of Jesus on your side—you are no longer defenseless. It's very common, even years down the road, to still have a vague sense of anxiety that may not be justified by your current circumstances. The only way to move beyond this fear is to face your fears head on and gain victory over them.

People who have experienced abuse will oftentimes try to prove themselves able to do good things. In the constant pursuit of being the best and being good, it is as if you are saying, "No one can have power over me. I can take care of myself. I am proving that I am not a bad person." At the same time, when you live in fear, you try to be invisible and stay in a safe place where no one will notice you. Also, you do not allow anyone to enter your world, nor would you allow the real you to come out.

Please list the things you fear and the people you fear:

_____

_____

_____

_____

_____

_____

Please take each fear that you listed and prayerfully give each one to God. Ask God to take these fears out of your heart and replace them with a spirit of boldness and courage. Let God know that you no longer want to run and hide. Tell Him you want to stand up and be counted.

Believe God for His protection, as well as His provision, in every area of your life. Commit yourself, your children, your job, your family, your income, and everything to Him. Only God can make anything you try to do of any value.

Please write Philippians 3:8:

_____

_____

_____

_____

Paul counts all things as rubbish, compared to knowing Christ.

Please write 1 John 4:18:

_____

_____

_____

_____

A healthy fear is to fear God, to stand in awe of Him, to be consumed with His presence in your life. Your fear of God will help you overcome your fear of the world. Beloved, stop hiding and living in fear. Trust God to bring about peace in your life. Please reflect on what God has already done to bring you to this point.

When you live with negative emotions, they become a mask that you hide behind to try and conceal all the hurt in your heart. I would like to encourage you to pray about removing the mask. Open and reveal your wounded heart to a friend who you feel is trustworthy. Share your past hurts and allow God to begin cleansing your heart. You're so brave!

This is the beginning of freedom for you!

PRAYER TIME

Holy Lord, I come before you with thanksgiving in my heart. Many times You have provided for me and my family, but I never thought to acknowledge You as the source of the provision. Please forgive me. Thank you for all the times You have provided for me. Thank you for loving me enough to provide the scraps from another's meal to nourish my body. Lord, please help me to be so in tune with You that I hear your still small voice say, "Put the leftovers in a freezer bag, for I know a hungry family who needs this nourishment." Father, I praise You for loving me enough to allow Your Son to be a living sacrifice for my sins. You did not provide an alternative offering. You gave me Your beautiful son, Jesus. Lord, may I not take this sacrifice in vain, but may I share Your incredible love with those I encounter and with those who do not know or understand how great Your love is for us all.

Father, please cleanse my heart of all the negative emotions I've carried around for so long. I want to manifest the fruits of the Spirit in my life found in Galatians 5:22-23: love, joy, peace, patience, kindness, goodness, faithfulness, gentleness, and self-control. In the name of Jesus, Amen.

it matters ...

On the Lake

The sun was just about to wake up and peep over the mini-mountain settled happily on the east side of the lake. Me, Dad, and my brother were in one boat, and my uncle and cousin were in another. We were racing over the smooth-as-glass lake to catch the first fish of the day. Just being in the boat as it cut through the still water excited me. Every time we were out to catch the next "big one" felt like a new adventure.

On this particular day, the boat slowed to a stop, we dropped the trolling motor into the water, and began casting our lines. No one made a sound for fear the fish would swim away. I liked to use a worm when I fished for bass. Whenever I slowly reeled in my line, I could tell when the worm would hit a log or something, but I could also tell when it was a fish ready to take a bite. You'd feel a bump, bump, and then you would know to pull the rod back quickly to try and hook the fish. Once it had taken the bait and you met some resistance, the battle was on. Would the fish work loose from the hook that had ensnared it, or would I be the victor and have the fish for dinner? This time I won. My prize: a nice largemouth bass. We continued fishing for a couple of hours. Suddenly, I heard a beaver slap its tail on the water—it sounded almost like a gunshot. Occasionally, we saw snakes slithering by on top of the water. Often, we would see a fish splash in the distance and watch rippling water fade away from the splash zone.

After we caught all the fish in the lake—not really, but this is my fish tale—we headed back to the cabin. As we neared it, we could smell bacon frying and biscuits baking. My mom and aunt were great cooks, but they learned everything they knew from Granny, who was in charge of breakfast. After we arrived inside the cabin and were seated to eat a delicious country meal complete with doodle-sop gravy, we told them all our fishing stories. We wanted to swim as soon as breakfast was over, but we had to wait at least thirty minutes for our food to settle. We got out of the water long enough to eat lunch, then got back in the water until dark.

On a different note, Dad taught us all how to ski. One summer we went to Cypress Gardens in Florida and watched their ski show, which featured skiers climbing on each other's shoulders to form a pyramid. Dad decided he wanted me, my brother, and my cousin to do something similar, but he had to concede that idea because I was in the mix. I could ski, but balancing, climbing, and lifting were not on the list of things I could do well. Instead, we skied three-up with different lengths in the ropes, with mine being longest and me being stationary, while my brother and cousin swept under the rope back and forth like little daredevils. Fun times! During the summer, we spent a lot of time at the lake. We loved being surrounded by family. Many times, there would be thirty other family members present. Dad taught them all to ski, and we ate well. My favorite childhood memories are right there on that lake with my family. That is where I felt safe and at home.

It matters that you have a place where you feel safe.

When I began writing my testimony in my book *Behind the Mask*, I realized that my favorite times were spent at the lake and that is where I wanted to live. I began searching for a home there, but the other person entered my life and interrupted my search. We had a whirlwind romance. We started dating December 3rd, got engaged January 29th, and eloped in a lovely little log cabin chapel that was nestled in the Great Smoky Mountains on March 4th. I lived in a little garden home community, and he moved in with me. We had talked about the possibility of buying some land, but I shared with him that I wanted to move to the lake, so we began our search for a home on the lake or some land. We were fortunate to find a home on the lake with a few acres of land. We moved into a fixer-upper, so every evening after work, we would work on the renovations. Come sunset, we'd go down to the pier to fish. That was my favorite time of day. We would sit and talk and catch fish. What more could a girl ask for?!

One night after fishing, I was cooking supper when I remembered that I had left something out at the pier. I grabbed a flashlight and went out the back door to retrieve the item when, suddenly, something caught my eye. I focused the flashlight on it. It was a scorpion at least five inches long, crawling with its tail up. I couldn't believe my eyes! I scanned for other scorpions, but spotted none. I walked up on the deck, picked up the cat's water bowl, and turned the bowl upside down over the scorpion, so it wouldn't run away. I ran inside to get the other person, who had just emerged from taking a shower.

"There's a giant scorpion out there that's this big," I said. I held out my thumb and pointer finger as far as they would stretch to reveal the length of the creature.

He shook his head and said, "There's no way, because scorpions that big don't live in this part of the world."

"I swear it's this big," I said and stretched out my fingers again. "You have got to come see it!"

We went outside to the overturned bowl. I stood several feet back and shined the flashlight on the bowl, while the other person lifted it up. He started laughing.

"You knucklehead, that's not a scorpion. It's a crawfish," he said.

Obviously, in all my lake adventures when I was a kid, we never went searching for crawfish. We were too busy swimming and skiing.

It matters that things aren't always what they seem to be.

After the divorce, I ended up staying in the lake house. I got the pontoon boat in the divorce, but I opted to sell it to pay bills. The other person got the bass boat, so I was stuck at the lake with no boat. It was totally no fun that summer—as far as being able to go out on the lake in a boat, anyway.

The next spring, a neighbor, who was moving, put her pontoon boat up for sale. I bought it. The last time I had driven a boat, I was a teenager. Since then, I had ridden in plenty of boats, but navigating and riding are different things. I arrived at my neighbor's home to pick up the boat, but neither one of us knew what to do. She knew that her husband, who had recently passed away, had added oil to the gas tank, but that was it. *How hard can this be?* I thought. I cranked up the boat, pulled out of the boathouse, and headed to the marina. I pulled up to the gas pump and parked the boat like a pro. I walked inside the marina and explained to the owner that I had no clue how to put oil in my boat. Thank God she really was an old pro. She knew exactly what to do. She told me how much oil to gas ratio I needed, so I took care of that and was off again. I felt free out on the lake in my very own boat that I drove all by myself. The lake became my Happy Place—it was peaceful. When I had a bad day at work or just needed to think and have some alone time, I would come home, get in my boat, and take off. I loved being out on the water—it refreshed me.

It matters that people are willing to help those in need.

I spend a lot of time with my grandchildren. They are the loves of my life, next to the Lord, who is my first love. With my grandchildren in mind, I decided it was time to buy a kayak. I thought it would be relaxing and peaceful just gliding along in the water, and I also thought a kayak would be a good source of exercise. Kayaking would be a fun thing we could do together.

One day, I went to look at a kayak a neighbor had for sale. I was definitely interested in it. He brought it over to my house and suggested that I try it out for a week before I committed to buying it. After he left, I stepped into the kayak to give it a try. As I started to sit down, I slipped and fell back onto the seat, and the kayak went floating off the ramp. Okay, that wasn't so bad, but my oar remained on the boat ramp. On this February day, I paddled with my arms in the chilly water to get back to the ramp. Finally, with oar in hand, I set off on my first kayaking adventure.

I paddled around in the cove where I live and explored the beaver trail. I'm not a beaver fan. They munch on my sea wall and eat my beautiful forsythia bushes. Now they're nothing but little nubbins. If I had my way, the beavers would be in beaver heaven. Okay, enough about beavers—back to the peaceful kayaking. I came close to a pterodactyl, better known as a blue heron, but it looks like a pterodactyl when it flies, so I renamed it. Happy little ducks swam around. I paddled past a muskrat doing whatever they do in the water. A fish splashed in the distance, and I passed a fisherman along the way. I headed back toward my house thinking how peaceful and enjoyable my kayaking adventure had been. Then I came upon the boat ramp. I tried to hold on to its edge to stand up. That didn't work— too wobbly. I tried backing up from it about ten feet to have a better shot at moving the kayak as far up the ramp as possible. I only got halfway. I tried again to stand up, but to no avail. My daughter, who was living with me, saw my dilemma and came out to offer a hand.

I handed my daughter the rope on the front of the kayak and asked her to pull me up the ramp. She pulled as far as she could, but I still only moved up halfway. I tried standing again and leaned over to grab the post, but into the water I went. When I came up out of the water, gasping because it was so cold, I saw my daughter was rolling on the ground from laughter. Life wouldn't be complete without a great kayaking adventure. I went and paid my neighbor for the kayak. I couldn't help myself. Once I told my grandchildren I bought it, they said, "Nanny, where's ours?" I now own three kayaks.

It matters that I fell into the cold water and my daughter got a good laugh at my expense.

POSITIVE WORD CONFESSIONS

"Make me know Thy ways, O Lord; teach me Thy paths. Lead me in Thy truth and teach me, for Thou art the God of my salvation; for Thee I wait all the day." *Psalm 25:4-5*

"Search me, O God, and know my heart; try me and know my anxious thoughts; and see if there be any hurtful way in me, and lead me in the everlasting way." *Psalm 139:23-24*

IN THE WORD

Do you have peace? As an adult, I never did because I never trusted anyone, plus I was a very prideful person. I also struggled with trusting God, because I was always striving to do things my own way, instead of waiting and listening for His still small voice. After some study in God's Word, I felt like the key to trusting God could be found in the word "humble." At first my thoughts were along the lines of, *What in the world does humble have to do with trusting God?* I was a very strong-willed, determined woman. I had no clue how to even begin to be humble, much less apply it to my relationship with God.

Please write James 4:6-7:

_____

_____

_____

_____

_____

Verse 6 indicates that God does not like proud people, but gives GRACE to the HUMBLE. I began to change my tune about becoming a HUMBLE person, because I like GRACE!

GRACE = Acceptance, Joy, Favor, Liberty

This single word put HUMBLE in a whole new light.

Verse 7 contains the word SUBMIT.

SUBMIT = OBEY; OBEY = To follow the commands or guidance of; to comply with.

Needless to say, I did not like the word SUBMIT any better than I liked HUMBLE. Can you relate? But guess what happens when you SUBMIT to God? Look at the last half of verse 7. When you SUBMIT to God, you have the authority to resist the devil so he will flee from you! Hallelujah!

Please read James 4:8.

God wants you to draw near to Him. To do so, He wants you to cleanse your hands and purify your heart. The more you cleanse and purify, the more intimate your relationship with God will become. You can cleanse yourself of the sin in your life and walk in God's ways, instead of the ways of the world—instead of your ways. God doesn't want you to be double-minded and desire the things of the world and the things of the Lord at the same time. There is no way you can ever be completely free from sin, because you are not perfect—only Jesus was perfect and died to save you from your sins. But you can make a daily choice to walk away from sin and not allow the devil to have a foothold in your life. You can SUBMIT to God. You can defend yourself from the attacks of the devil. How? By putting on the full armor of God.

Please read Ephesians 6:10-18, and list the seven pieces of spiritual armor (verses 14-18) God provides for us to put on daily:

1.

2.

3.

4.

5.

6.

7.

Ephesians 6:11 mentions the word "schemes." What schemes? This word clearly labels the assaults against Christians as well as thought-out plans of attack, like something a terrorist might devise—very deadly and very serious. I prayed and asked God to show me why this spiritual armor He provides for our protection is so important to put on every day.

I decided to take a break from writing and swim for a while. I put SPF 30 sunscreen all over my body, because I have fair skin. I was out in the sun for a couple of hours, came back in, and started writing again. Initially, the effectiveness of the sunscreen impressed me, but after a while I noticed some red spots along the edge of my swimsuit and on my back that I hadn't been able to reach with the sunscreen. These areas had been unprotected from the sun. So guess what happened? I got burned!

God revealed to me that this is what happens to Christians when we go into spiritual battle unprotected or without all our armor on—we get burned spiritually. The devil will find that one small spot that is left unprotected and will attack it. So I want to encourage you to learn how to put on the Full Armor of God and wear it daily. Let's explore the armor:

The Girdle of Truth
The girdle was the basic piece of military equipment the soldier used during war. It enabled the soldier to use the whole armor effectively. It also protected the lower part of the torso and held the sword.

Please write John 14:6:

_____

_____

_____

_____

When you put on the Girdle of Truth, you are basically putting on Jesus. Without having a relationship with Jesus, no one can enter into spiritual warfare with any prospect of success. As you move forward into battle, you know that truth will prevail and as you walk in truth, speak truth, and live a truthful live, it will help you to not be double-minded.

Please write James 1:6-8:

_____

_____

_____

_____

_____

The Breastplate of Righteousness

This piece of armor covered the soldier's body and protected the heart and other vital organs from being injured during battle. It would be equivalent to today's bulletproof vest.

The word "righteousness" used to describe the breastplate is interesting, because we know that only one man in history was deemed righteous by God and that is our Lord and Savior Jesus Christ. How can you put on the Breastplate of Righteousness? The only way is to accept the sacrifice of death, which Jesus, who deserved no death Himself, offered on your behalf.

As you meditate upon God's Word, realize this righteousness. Christ's blood applied to your life defines everything upon which your spiritual existence depends. If you possess this gift of righteousness through Christ, you have an impenetrable defense against the attacks of the devil, because your life in Christ is guarded and protected by His righteousness. Seek Him first and foremost in all things.

Please write Matthew 6:33:

_____

_____

_____

The Shoes of Peace

A soldier wore sandals that were usually made with metal cleats attached to the bottom to make him more surefooted in battle. Shod is believed by some scholars to be a metal shield that protected the soldier's shins from any gall-traps or sharp sticks that might have been laid in the field by the enemy to obstruct the soldier's marching.

The Christian life can bring about peace with God, peace with self, and peace with others. This peace does not mean you will never encounter any obstacles or have frustrating days, but that you will have peace in the midst of these frustrations. You can spread the peace of God to others with your Shoes of Peace.

Please write Romans 10:14-15:

_____

_____

_____

_____

The Shield of Faith

Paul says "Above all." Do you think that Paul may have felt faith is the Christian's most important defense and the most important piece of the armor? The shield could be turned to confront an attack from any direction. Some believe this piece of armor was an oblong shield that covered the soldier's entire body when in battle.

The devil is ready to shoot his fiery arrows when you least expect it. He waits for the most opportune moment to attack. When you lower your shield and think nothing will happen, that's when you will get hit with temptation.

Please read Ephesians 6:16 and write out how many darts God gives us the ability to quench by putting on the full armor of God: _____

ALL!

Please write Psalm 3:3:

_____

_____

_____

_____

Please write Psalm 28:7:

_____

_____

_____

_____

The Helmet of Salvation

Soldiers wore helmets, the primary protection against the lethal blow of a battle-axe. The helmets also served another function. Like a modern-day football helmet, symbols adorned them that identified the army of the soldier.

Do you want the cross of Christ to be the symbol on your Helmet of Salvation?

I believe your mind is the devil's primary target, because anyone who has a double-mind will be unstable in all their ways. The devil will even try to put thoughts in your mind to make you doubt your salvation. The following experience happened when I was a baby Christian:

One day at work while trying to assist a customer on a phone call, he asked me, "Are you saved?" "I'm working on it," I responded. In a loud, gruff voice, he said, "Working on it?

Either you are or you're not!" That got me to thinking, *Am I really saved? Am I a Christian?* I had asked Jesus into my heart, but was that good enough? Was there something else I needed to do? It's just like the devil to put all these doubtful thoughts in my mind, but at the time I didn't fully understand what a conniving manipulator the devil could be. I prayed and asked God, *Am I really saved?*

That night, I had a dream. This dream occurred for seven consecutive nights. The first night, I was at a snack-bar-kind-of place on the top of a hill by a lake. There was a covered patio area where you could get your food, sit down, and eat at a picnic table. In this dream, I went down to the water. At its edge, a pier jutted out from the land in the shape of a T. Bright orange buoys were tied to the end of the pier, and when I looked beyond the buoys, I no longer saw a lake. I saw an endless ocean. People were jumping off the pier, while others were being pushed off it. If they swam past the end of the buoys, they were saved. I know this sounds strange, but this was the dream God gave me.

In this recurring dream, each night I would walk down to the side of the pier and watch people. Some were saved, some were not. On the seventh night of the dream, I was up at the snack bar on the telephone when Mom came up and tapped me on the shoulder and said, "It's time." I hung up the phone, turned around, and instead of picnic tables as in the previous night's dreams, I saw pews. All the people who had been sitting at the picnic tables before were now situated on the front pew. As I walked by, they shook my hand. With concerned looks, each person said, "I hope you're saved." I walked to the end of the pier, jumped in, and swam beyond the end of the buoys. I was saved. Since that night, I have never doubted my salvation. Beloved, if you are in a place today where you are doubting your salvation, please pray and ask God to confirm your salvation. Your confirmation may not be in the form of a dream like mine, but God will not leave you in doubt.

The Sword of the Spirit

The sword was used for close attack by the soldier. Just as the sword was a necessary part of the soldier's equipment, the Word of God is a very necessary part of your equipment as a Christian. The Word enables you to answer attacks on your faith as well as make sure your everyday decisions are compatible with the Word of God. It will guide and comfort, encourage and strengthen. The Word of God is truly a powerful weapon.

Please read Luke 4:1-13:

In each instance when Jesus was tempted by the devil, Jesus responded, "It is written!" *(verses 4, 8, and 12)*

Jesus threw the Word of God back at the devil in response to the devil's temptations.

You have that same power to use the Word as a weapon against the attacks of the devil. Do you know why it is so important to study the Word? So when you are tempted, you can recall a verse of Scripture and tell the devil, "It is written!"

Please write Hebrews 4:12:

_____

_____

_____

_____

_____

Prayer

Once the Armor of God is on, the soldier is fully equipped and goes to his commanding officer to obtain the battle plans. This is what every Christian does as they seek the Lord in prayer. He is your commanding officer. God's Word commands you to not only pray for yourself, but to pray for all the saints going into battle each day. "With all prayer and petition pray at all times in the Spirit, and with this in view, be on the alert with all perseverance and petition for all the saints" *(Eph. 6:18)*.

When you get in your prayer closet, you can express your adoration to God. You can praise Him, you can confess your sins to Him, you can thank Him in advance for answered prayers, you can express your need of Him, you can ask for things you need, you can intercede on behalf of others, and you can pray for the salvation of those who do not know Jesus as their Savior.

Even in the most difficult times, you can have the assurance that God is working on your behalf for your ultimate good.

Please write Philippians 1:6:

_____

_____

_____

_____

_____

PRAYER TIME

Father, I live in a world full of constant chaos, and I need Your peace. Please give me the will to want to humble myself before You, that I may be able to submit my life to Your ways, Your truth, and Your life. I need to know how to resist the devil so he will flee from me. Help me, Lord!

In the name of Jesus, I put on the Girdle of Truth, that I may speak truth in all circumstances and know that any tongue which rises against me will be shown to be in the wrong. I put on the Breastplate of Righteousness to protect my heart. Father, please help me keep my heart pure and clean, so I may be always in tune to hear Your still small voice. I put on the Helmet of Salvation. Father, help me be mindful of the things that I see and hear that go into my mind. When someone at the office is gossiping, give me the will to turn around and walk away. When someone wants to go see an inappropriate movie, please give me the will to say "no." When something comes on the television, online, or on the radio that will negatively influence my thoughts, please give me the will to turn it off. I put on the Shoes of Peace, so I can go and share the love of Jesus with others. Thank you for preparing their hearts to receive Jesus as their Savior. I take up the Shield of Faith in knowing that You, Lord, are going before me into battle and Your angels encamp around me to fight with me and for me. I take up the Sword of the Spirit, Your Word. Please give me a hunger and thirst for Your Word, that I may refute the devil as Jesus did and say, "It is written!" In the name of Jesus, Amen!

it matters ...
That You Spread the Gospel

I love to help others—my parents instilled this desire into each one of us kids. While I had my own ministry helping women overcome the hurts of having had an abortion, I enjoyed getting involved in other ministry opportunities through my church, particularly the inner-city ministry. We would go into a rough section of Birmingham and share the Gospel through Bible studies, drama skits for the kids, hot dog cookouts, or just shooting some hoops—whatever it took.

One Saturday, guys from our drug and alcohol recovery ministry, regular inner-city helpers, and evangelism group members all pitched in to make a communitywide event at an inner-city church a success. A friend and I in the evangelism group were known as The Confronters. We acquired this name while in a year-long School of Ministry program that equipped us to be better ministers of the Gospel. There, it was determined that we were not afraid to share the Gospel under any circumstances. I learned a lot through this ministry and made some good friends.

Early in the day, we did games and crafts with the kids. Later, we held a big cookout for the community and served a gazillion hot dogs, chips, drinks, and cookies. We ended the day by evangelizing in a local housing project. Souls were won into the Kingdom, and we felt very blessed to have been a part of the outreach. I got in my car, along with several friends. I turned the key to crank the car, nothing happened—not even a little spark. Tried again—nothing. It was starting to get dark. This was not the greatest place to be at night. I got out of the car and walked over to the guy who had led our group. I explained that my car was completely dead. Another guy tried to crank it—nothing. Our leader lifted the hood of the car, anointed the engine with oil, and said, "Let's all join hands and pray." The whole team circled my car and our leader began to pray, with all of us agreeing with him in prayer. After the prayer, one of the guys got in my car, turned the key, and it cranked right up! Hallelujah!

It matters that we go and share the Good News with others.

Being in ministry work, people and churches lent me financial support—they provided material to those who could not afford to purchase it, covered ministry costs, etc. I was considered an in-state missionary. One of the churches that supported me sent me an invitation, along with numerous other missionaries from around the world who were home on furlough, to attend a Christmas party. The party was very nicely done and very festive. We ate, laughed, and shared our ministry work with each other, so we could be in prayer for each other throughout the coming year.

As soon as I shared that I had been the director of a crisis pregnancy center (CPC) and director of an abortion recovery ministry, a woman who served as a missionary in Ukraine came up to me, grabbed me by the arms, started shaking me, and said, "You've got to come to Ukraine! You've got to come to Ukraine! Every other baby is aborted over there. You've got to come!"

Come to find out, she and her husband had been missionaries in Ukraine for the past fifteen years. They were home on furlough to visit family for Christmas, then they would be heading back to Ukraine. She explained that abortions are free there, because it is a second world country. Instead of purchasing contraceptives, women would get an abortion as a form of birth control, she informed me. She shared with me about a lady there who wanted to establish a CPC and wanted to know if I would consider traveling to Ukraine to help her train the volunteers and teach abortion recovery.

Wow!

I had never contemplated leaving the United States, but I assured her I would definitely pray about this mission opportunity. She gave me her contact information and promised to keep in touch. I prayed about it. I sent out a newsletter explaining this opportunity, how much it would cost, and asked if anyone would be interested in helping fund the trip. Within two weeks, I received half of the money I needed to make the trip and still had six months left to raise/ save the rest of the funds. I began attending the monthly Ukraine mission trip meetings. Through them, I discovered that I would be traveling with a local church that supported several orphanages in Ukraine, an abandoned baby hospital, and a church in Izmail, Ukraine.

On a balmy July day at five a.m., our team flew from Birmingham to Dulles International Airport in Virginia. From there we flew to Vienna, Austria, and then to Odessa, Ukraine. Upon arriving in Ukraine, we boarded a bus and spent the next five hours traveling to Izmail. Overall, we had traveled for thirty-six hours.

For some reason when I think of Ukraine, I think cold. Well, it wasn't cold at all. An unusual heatwave was sweeping through the country—one hundred five degrees Fahrenheit! Upon our arrival in Izmail, people from the local church greeted us. Then we checked into our respective hotel rooms and found that they were nice and clean, but hot. In my room, I immediately walked over to the window unit and turned it on. I waited for the cold air to begin blowing, but the unit only forced out lukewarm air. Apparently, they didn't believe in charging their air conditioners with Freon here.

I showered, then I plugged in my hairdryer and in what seemed like a minute, it turned red and blew up! In our monthly meetings we'd been told to bring plug adapters, but no one had said anything about a voltage adapter—or if they had, I'd had no clue what they were talking about. Good thing I had a window unit—suddenly, it became my makeshift hairdryer!

After I got myself ready, I went to one of the larger rooms to dine with my fellow missionaries, then we all returned to our own rooms for some much-needed sleep. But sleeping with sweat dripping down our necks, back, and everywhere in between was hard. During our monthly mission meetings, we had been given a list of things to bring on the trip. Two of the items were eye covers and earplugs. I did not know why I'd need them, but I'd brought them anyway.

Our first night in Izmail, we learned that it did not get dark until ten p.m.—and the sun rose bright and early at three a.m.! As soon as the sun was up, so were all the town workers. With it being so hot and no air, our windows were open, so we could hear everything going on outside. We all slept with the doors and windows of our rooms wide open in hopes that we might get a breeze blowing from room to room. We were too hot to care if anyone killed us in our sleep, plus our team occupied the entire second floor of the small hotel.

Each day started off with a Ukrainian breakfast, complete with scrambled eggs, bacon, sausage, and toast. They wanted us to feel at home, so they made us what they thought we would normally have had for breakfast in the States. Their menu would have been completely different. After breakfast, we would settle into the courtyard of a flat complex, same as an apartment complex here, and we played musical instruments. Soon, kids who lived in the complex would come out exploring. The first day we ministered, with our interpreters, to about twenty kids during our makeshift Vacation Bible School (VBS) and by the end of the week, more than a hundred children were attending our VBS.

Each day after lunch, we explored the ministries the church supported—the orphanages and abandoned baby hospital. One day we took a two-hour trip to visit an orphanage by the Black Sea. We entertained the kids with a drama skit, shared the Gospel, and had a great time. Along the way, we came upon thousands of acres of sunflowers—one of the most beautiful sights I have ever seen. The sunflowers were upward of six feet tall. I can't even begin to describe their beauty.

At night, while the team went out to eat and explore the town, I trained the volunteers who wanted to start a CPC. It was rather slow going, because I had to use an interpreter, but the information I imparted was well received. After the training, I took a taxi back to the hotel. I had a card printed on light blue paper with the hotel address printed in bright red ink. I hailed a taxi, showed the card to the driver, and got in to experience the ride of my life. Apparently, there are no driving laws in this area of Ukraine, or I had a maniac driver each night—one of the two. I felt like I was in the backseat of a car driven by Mario Andretti. Good thing I didn't get car sick. To add to the maniac driving, the streets were littered with potholes. Each night as the driver rounded the corner to the hotel and came to a screeching halt at the front door, I jumped out as quickly as possible, handed him the equivalent of a twenty dollar bill, and he sped away. Come to find out at the end of the week, I was giving the drivers about ten times the cost of the taxi ride. Live and learn.

Our last night in Ukraine, we hiked about a mile out into the woods to have a picnic. The people from the church, who by this time had become our friends, dug several holes in the ground, filled them with charcoal, and roasted skewers of meat. We had gotten to know the people from the church very well and they had each brought a dish to share with us. We sat on the ground on picnic blankets, shared our love of our Lord with one another, shared our lives, and ate well. One of the guys on our team encouraged me to eat a piece of cornbread. After I took a bite, he and several team members started laughing. One of them whispered in my ear that I had just eaten ants. I looked down at the cornbread. Sure enough, ants were sprinkled throughout it. Come to find out, one of the elderly women in the church, who couldn't see well, had brought the cornbread. Apparently, she had an ant problem at home. They had also eaten the cornbread, so they were just sharing the love.

We ended the evening standing and singing "Amazing Grace" in our own language, and it was so beautiful! By the end of the song, not an eye was dry. The next day, we headed back home. I left part of my heart with those amazing people of God. To this day, I still keep in contact with some of them. That trip will probably go down in my book as one of the coolest things I'll ever have the opportunity to be a part of. Praise God!

It matters that every other baby is
killed by abortion in Ukraine.
It matters that three thousand babies
are killed by abortion each day in the USA.

One day at church, I noticed a post in the bulletin about a mission trip to the Amazon. I imagined it as an exotic getaway. *It would really be cool to go somewhere like that,* I thought.

Quickly, I dismissed the thought, but then each week I would see it in the bulletin and felt God tugging at my heartstrings to go on this trip. After I learned that a mission meeting was set, I attended it to learn who would be leading the trip and what the mission's goal would be. If the aim was to build things, I wouldn't be going. Once, I volunteered with Habitat for Humanity to paint the inside of a house. The Habitat people tell you to bring extra tools in case you might need something or want to get involved with another project, so I had brought my toolbox that contained my hammer and screwdrivers and I had also brought my paint equipment.

I arrived on the scene, and organizers announced that the house we were to work on had been completed the day before. Naturally, I was bummed, because I like to help people and I like to paint. This burley lookin' fellow came up to me and asked, "Little Lady, do you know how to use a hammer?" I nodded yes. He instructed me to follow him and several others to another house. We followed, but ultimately, there was no house—only a foundation. Several other ladies and I gathered around this guy, who told us we would be framing a house. We all laughed, but he cut us short when he said, "Let's get at it!" I'm always up for a great adventure, so I was all about trying something new. He marked where the nails needed to be hammered, and we all went at it, as instructed. Well anyway, in my opinion, if you've framed one house, you've framed them all. Why bother doing that again?

At the Amazon mission meeting that afternoon, the leader revealed the upcoming trip would be a medical mission with doctors and nurses administering aid to the sick people in the villages. Further, she explained that they needed help with counseling and sharing the Gospel with the adults in the villages and also needed help with the children. I knew exactly where I was needed on this trip—ministering to the adults. That's what I do every day. It's right up my alley.

The leader asked us to pray about what God would have us do on this trip and said we would discuss it at the next mission meeting. I began praying, and a few days later, God spoke to my heart and said, "I want you to be in charge of the children's ministry." I laughed and said, "No, God. I don't think that is where I would best utilize my ministry skills." I kept praying. Once again, God spoke to my heart and said, "I want you to oversee the children's ministry." I replied, "Okay, God. Please confirm that for me, so I will know we're on the same page here." The next week as I walked through the door to attend the mission meeting, the leader immediately approached me and said, "Amy, I want you to pray about doing something on the mission trip." I replied, "Sure, what would you like for me to do?" She replied, "I want you to oversee the children's ministry." Done! I think God gets a good laugh at me sometimes. I explained to the leader that her request was a confirmation, so I knew I needed to be on this Amazon mission trip and lead the children's ministry.

I had a general idea of what needed to be done and had a little experience working with the VBS kids during the Ukraine trip a few years before. We had only so much room to take extra items, so I limited my toys to whistles, paper, crayons, pencils, sharpeners, soccer balls, bubbles, toothbrushes and toothpaste, Gospel bracelet makers, stuff to make crosses, wooden airplanes, cute little Gospel pictures with Spanish words on them for the kids to color—you get the general idea. Just a bunch of fun little things for the kids. I had everything organized and all the boxes numbered for which day of the trip we would need the supplies. Also, each team member had a numbered box to pack in their luggage.

We arrived in Lima, Peru, went through customs, and spent the night in a local hotel. It was neat to stay in the city and see how the people lived. Most of the buildings were very brightly painted and beautifully designed. That evening we traveled to the outskirts of the city to eat dinner at a restaurant overlooking the Pacific Ocean. The next day we flew to Iquitos, Peru, where we boarded a big houseboat that would take us to the villages where we were to minister. Two people were in each room, and each room had a set of bunk beds, a small bathroom with a shower, and was not over two hundred square feet, but had an air conditioner.

The man who owned the boat explained that there would be no hot water in the showers. One afternoon, I stood in the bathroom waiting for the water to warm up when I realized it wasn't going to get any better. I braved the cold and jumped in. Of course, we were in the Amazon rainforest and it was scorching hot outside, so the cold water wasn't so bad. A chef on the boat cooked breakfast, lunch, and dinner. The authentic Peruvian dishes were wonderful, and the eating area was also air conditioned—we really roughed it on the Amazon River. We spent that evening traveling down the river to our first village. It was much like being on a river in the United States, but the currents were very swift. A pink dolphin followed our boat for a while. I wanted to see an anaconda, but missed out on that. Probably a good thing. The entire area was a tropical paradise to us Alabamians. While we see bluebirds and sparrows sitting in trees in Alabama, we saw beautiful, brightly colored parrots flying in the Amazon rainforest.

Village One—We arrived at the first village bright and early the next day and saw people arriving by boat to receive medical aid. People's homes were, as you would imagine, built with thatched siding and roofs and most were on piers. A lady swept the dirt floor of a thatch-covered building. We saw some cement block buildings—the school house and the church, which were also covered with a thatched roof and painted on the outside.

A lone sidewalk meandered through the village, and the houses stood around a soccer field. Excellent place to pick up a great soccer player. All those on our team who had the children's boxes marked with a one brought them to the team meeting. We had a prayer time before we exited the boat to go into the village to begin ministering. The doctors, nurses, and counselors set up their stations to see patients, who needed physical and spiritual healing, while my people and I set up for the kids. We broke out a jug of bubbles and began blowing. The younger kids chased the bubbles and squealed with delight as they tried to catch them. The older kids came out to see what the younger kids were up to.

We broke out the interpreters and rounded up the kids, who were absolutely beautiful, well-mannered, and eager to learn. Right before lunchtime, we handed them whistles. They ran around everywhere blowing them. They were so cute! A short time later, one of the counselors stood in the door of the school building where we were ministering. His face was grim, and he had placed his hands on his hips. I looked at him and said, "What?" He said, "We can't even hear a heartbeat out here."

Oops! Mental note to self: Save whistles to the end of the day next time.

Village Two—Same as day one, but we finished earlier and took a three-mile hike through the Amazon rainforest. I put my hiking boots on and sprayed insect repellant all over me—I was ready for a great hiking adventure. Our guide explained the medicinal purposes of the plants and trees and how some trees were used to create different-colored dyes. They actually have students attend the local university to learn how to be rainforest guides. He picked up a poisonous frog and asked if we wanted to hold it. No one accepted his invitation. On the hike, we swung on vines and trekked through deep mud. When we made it back to the boat, we were all covered in sweat and bugs and knee deep in mud, but we had a really cool adventure. This particular village had a policeman, villagers who made crafts, and a monkey named Alexandria. She hung out in the rafters above the medical and counseling teams. One young man gave me a piranha necklace made with different-sized painted seeds and featuring the jaws of a piranha. The necklace was beautiful! Piranha fish taste yummy too—just for the record. Another young man gave me a lovely bracelet made of colored seeds and twine. I still have both gifts and wouldn't part with them.

Village Three—Same as day one, but this village had a Shaman, what is better known as a witchdoctor. After our ministry time that day, the team wanted to go to the Shaman's house to lay hands on a sick man. I get the laying on of hands, but I did not like the notion of being in the presence of a witch doctor. I just knew there was a Scripture about not associating with evil, so I remained on the boat. That was a great adventure I was willing to forfeit.

Village Four—This village was like an upscale tropical paradise. All the villages were very exotic, but this was one you would want to escape to and never leave. A swinging bridge extended over the creek below, and giant palm trees and tropical plants were everywhere. This particular day, it was raining—not just a drizzle, but a downpour. It seems people in the Amazon rainforest don't like to venture out when it's raining. Go figure. We saw a few brave souls that day, and we ministered to a few kids. One of the team doctors told me he had never seen a children's ministry so organized as mine. That made me feel good. We shared the Gospel, souls were saved, people were baptized in the Amazon River, others received medical attention—mission accomplished. Through this time of ministry with the kids, God reaffirmed to me that we may have different skin colors and we may speak different languages, but we all have the same need—to be loved by God and others, to be ministered to, and to let the smile of a beautiful child brighten our day.

It matters that you listen to God's still
small voice and not miss out on a blessing.

POSITIVE WORD CONFESSIONS

"If I speak with the tongues of men and of angels, but do not have love, I have become a noisy gong or a clanging cymbal." *1 Corinthians 13:1*

"The Lord is my strength and song, and He has become my salvation." *Psalm 118:14*

IN THE WORD

If you are going to trust someone, you want to get to know the one in whom you are putting your trust. When you trust someone, you are putting your confidence in that person. You may have an easier time trusting a person, because you have invested time getting to know them. What about God. Do you trust Him? To begin trusting God, establish a relationship with Him. I want to share a verse with you that really helped me persevere in my journey to learn how to trust God. "It is better to take refuge in the Lord than to trust in man" *(Ps. 118:8)*. For years, I had this all backward. I would trust people, but not trust God.

Please list beside each verse the benefit of trusting God:

Psalm 5:11 _____

Psalm 22:4-5 _____

Psalm 25:2-3 _____

Psalm 32:10 _____

Psalm 40:4 _____

Psalm 56:4 _____

Proverbs 3:5-6 _____

Please list the things you should **NOT** put your trust in beside each verse:

Psalm 44:6 _____

Psalm 49:6-7 _____

Psalm 146:3 _____

Jeremiah 17:5 _____

Jeremiah 48:7 _____

Ezekiel 33:13 _____

Please write 1 John 4:19:

_____
_____
_____
_____
_____

When you know someone loves you, it's easier to trust them. God has loved you first. You are a responder to the love He extends to you. He is your Abba Father. God wants to fellowship with you through prayer. He wants to love you! He wants to wipe away your tears, if you will just let Him near. There is nothing you can say or do to make Him love you. He loves you just the way you are. Run into His arms and receive His love. Relax in Him knowing you can trust Him. God will not hurt you. Trust Him, and take refuge in Him.

WISDOM

You just looked at reasons why you should trust God, and you looked at things you should not trust. To apply your trust appropriately, you must make wise choices.

Please read James 3:13-18, and list the characteristics of Worldly (verses 14-16) wisdom and Heavenly (verses 17-18) below:

WORLDLY:

_____

_____

_____

_____

HEAVENLY:

_____

_____

_____

_____

Which wisdom do you prefer? Wisdom is something you should pray for every day. I pray Colossians 1:9-14 over me and everyone I pray for on a daily basis and have for years. The book of Proverbs is full of wisdom Scriptures. It outlines how important it is to have wisdom—to be desired above all riches, because nothing can compare to wisdom. God's Word even refers to wisdom as a "her." "Wisdom shouts in the street, she lifts her voice in the square; at the head of the noisy streets she cries out; at the entrance of the gates in the city, she utters her sayings" *(Prov. 1:20-21)*. Two other words that are synonymous with wisdom are "understanding" and "knowledge."

Please read the following verses and fill in the blanks:

Proverbs 1:5 "A wise man will hear and increase in learning, and a man of _____ will acquire wise counsel."

Proverbs 2:6 "For the Lord gives _____; from His mouth come _____ and _____."

Proverbs 3:13 "How blessed is the man who finds _____, and the man who gains _____."

Proverbs 3:19-20 "The Lord by _____ founded the earth; by _____ He established the heavens. By His _____ the deeps were broken up, and the skies drip with dew."

Proverbs 8:11 "For _____ is better than jewels; and all desirable things can not compare with her."

Proverbs 16:16 "How much better it is to get _____ than gold! And to get _____ is to be chosen above silver."

James 1:5 "But if any of you lacks _____, let him ask of God, who gives to all men generously and without reproach, and it will be given to him."

Whenever you are struggling to make a wise decision, just ask yourself WWJD (What Would Jesus Do)?

Let's look further to see what Jesus would do.

Please read Matthew 11:28-30.

Jesus wants you to get yoked up with Him. What does this mean? A yoke is a bar of wood constructed to unite two animals to work in the fields. Yoked animals work side by side until the yoke is removed. Jesus wants you yoked with him, so as you go through life you will not get weary and burdened. Jesus will be there to help you carry the load. You're not alone. Can you imagine what it would be like to walk side by side with Jesus?

Please read the following Scriptures, and note what you learned from Jesus:

John 13:12-17 _____

Ephesians 4:17-24 _____

Philippians 2:5-11 _____

1 Peter 2:21-24 _____

1 John 2:1-6 _____

In light of all you have just read, please describe how you would live, day by day, yoked with Jesus:

_____
_____
_____
_____
_____
_____

PRAYER TIME

Holy Father, I want to be in tune with You to hear Your still small voice and know when I need to take advantage of a mission trip or be involved in a local ministry. I want to love others the way You love them. When I doubt, please confirm Your will for my life. Please help me focus on Your heavenly wisdom and cast away the wisdom of the world. I want to have a heart that totally trusts You. Help me to yoke up with Jesus and walk with Him in this journey of life. Thank you for not giving up on me. Thank you for guiding me down the path You have planned for me. Thank you for helping me understand my purpose in this mixed up, crazy life on earth. Lord, I need You! In the name of Jesus, Amen.

it matters ...
Hanging Out with Friends

A few years after my divorce, I was bored and needed friends, so I decided to join a singles group at a large church in Birmingham. The church's website featured groups of singles looking for fellowship just like me. I signed up with a hiking group. I had not hiked in years and thought it would be nice to smell the fresh air while getting some good exercise during a leisurely hike through the mountains.

The week before the hike, I journeyed to my parents' house for a family get together. As we sat around the table eating lunch, I announced that I had joined a singles hiking group at church. Instead of encouragement, a roar of laughter erupted. My oldest brother said first, "Don't go." Then my sister suggested I tell them I was sick. Mom, well, she was still laughing so hard she couldn't speak.

Okay, so I'm not the most sure-footed person in the world. "Jeez," I told them. "It's just a little hike."

Saturday came, and I put on a pair of shorts and a top, along with a good supportive pair of athletic shoes. I was trying to look as cute as possible, because there would be single guys at the hike. I arrived at the park and began introducing myself. Then our leader announced which trail we would hike and offered up a prayer. We were off.

We began ascending the first mini-mountain. What I thought would be a happy leisurely hike was more like a marathon sprint to see how quickly we could get to the top of this mountain. Apparently, our leader wasn't into enjoying the scenery. Well, I was not going to let anyone think I was a wimp, so I huffed and puffed up the trail. Finally, I had to stop for a minute to catch my breath. Actually, it wasn't even a minute because that would have thrown off the entire hike schedule. By the time we reached our first resting spot, sweat dripped off me from head to toe. I was completely out of breath. The leader announced that we would begin the ascent of the next mini-mountain and everyone needed to keep up.

Okay, why didn't he just say, *Amy, step it up, sister!* I can take a hint.

We began the ascent, and it wasn't any easier doing the marathon trek up this mini-mountain than it was the other one. On the way down the mountain, I stepped wrong and twisted my ankle a little bit, but no big deal. I was not a wimp. We finally arrived at a level place where we were about to rest again, and secretly I was counting my blessings that I had not passed out yet. I was looking around and enjoying the beautiful scenery when, suddenly, down I went.

I had tripped over the root of a tree growing in the middle of the path. One of the guys ran over to me and told me to stay put. An intense pain radiated from my knee, my ankles, my shoulder, and my wrist—okay, my whole body hurt. I had a flashback to my family laughing at me. I thought, *Why didn't I listen to the those who know me best?* The leader came over to make sure I wasn't dead. I asked if the hike was almost over, and he said we were only halfway done—we had another two miles to go. I groaned and thought, *Just get a gun and put me down.* I tried to get up, but failed. A few of the hikers helped me to finally get on my feet. All the while I was still trying to maintain the "I'm not a wimp" mentality. I hobbled over to the leader. I had twisted my ankles, blown out my knee, and hurt my wrist pretty bad. Oh, and let's not forget that my shoulder was hurting too. I was trying to determine if I should ask them to send a chopper to rescue me, but decided against that.

The leader told me I could wait at a lake while they hiked, or I could continue to hike and they would slow down so I could keep up. That was a very nice gesture, so I agreed to keep going. He gave me his walking stick to help me out. As our group hiked around the lake, I didn't enjoy it as much as I would have if I were not injured, but it was nice nonetheless. Plus, I was really surprised by how many nice people had stayed behind and hiked with a cripple. We got to a point in the hike where we would ascend a hill, and the leader suggested that I take a shortcut to the cars. He was probably tired of walking slow and wanted to get rid of me. A couple of the girls wanted to go with me for support. We finally made it to our cars. I drove home, and later, as I entered my house, I cried and said, "I am a wimp. No more hiking for me!"

It matters that I was injured and others wanted to help me.

Obviously, the hiking group was not my thing, so I got involved with another singles group at the church. This one took ballroom dance classes. We also had game nights and were always going out to eat and getting together to do other fun things. We also supported a local charity, and to help it raise money, we put together a team to compete in a dragon boat race. A dragon boat is long, narrow, and seats ten rows of two people, with a drummer person in the bow and a person at the stern. As newbie dragon boat racers, we needed an experienced person to steer, so we would not run over the other boaters in the race. We recruited twenty-one people from our singles group, and each of us paid seventy-five dollars to the charity for the honor to compete in the race. The Friday night before the event, we all met and carpooled fifty miles to train. I drove myself and two others.

We arrived at the race location, donned life jackets, and headed to our boat to practice. The boat "seats" were a two-by-four board stretched across the width of the boat, wide enough for two average-sized butts and no extra. We paddled around for an hour and learned the techniques of the race. You have to put just the tip of your paddle in the water, and when you hear the whistle, everyone paddles. When the drummer hits the drum, your team is supposed to have its paddle back in the water for another stroke.

After an hour sitting on the two-by-four, we were ready for some dinner and ate at the restaurant by the river. That night, the place featured a band and ballroom dancing. Some of our group stayed, while the friends who had come over with me were ready to head home. We'd had a long day at work. On the way back, we talked about how difficult it is to find someone you're compatible with and how do you know when you've found "the one." I shared with my two passengers—a male and a female—that I knew of an article that encourages you and a potential partner to ask each other a specific set of questions that are supposed to make you fall in love. So we decided to quiz each other with the questions I remembered.

By the time we reached my companions' cars, we all knew a lot more about each other, but neither of us girls were in love with the guy, and he wasn't in love with either of us. Well, it may be because we had not gazed into each other's eyes for four minutes like the article instructed. Anyway, we woke up bright and early the next day and met at the same carpool spot. My male friend asked me if I had changed my mind about being in love with him. "No," I said. We laughed.

We drove back to the dragon boat race and arrived to a throng of people. There were thirty-two race teams, with eight teams in each category. Each heat consisted of four boats with four categories of racers: 1) Nonprofit, 2) Community, 3) College, and 4) Business. We were on the Community team. The top sixteen winners would race again, then the four winners of those heats would race for the top four positions. Our team donned our jackets and got in our boat. As soon as I sat, I realized I had an imprint of the two-by-four on my butt from the hour-long training the night before. My butt was very sore. *Oh well*, I thought, *this is for a good cause and for the pleasure of being around lots of fun people—plus I'm not a wimp.*

We got out on the water, got into position with the other three boats, and the whistle sounded. We paddled as fast as we could. We came in second. That was good enough for us to race again. We ate lunch and hung out to watch the other boats compete, then we were back up. We donned our life jackets and got into our boat. My butt was still sore. We came in second again, but that was not good enough to move on to the final round. We had a great time that day, though! We placed fifteenth overall, which was not so bad considering we were newbies at the sport.

It matters that you find "the one" you're supposed to be with and have fun with friends while you're waiting.

POSITIVE WORD CONFESSIONS

"This is the day which the Lord has made; let us (I will) rejoice and be glad in it." *Psalm 118:24*

"(I will) Trust in the Lord, and do good; (I will) Dwell in the land and cultivate faithfulness. (I will) Delight yourself (myself) in the Lord, and He will give you (me) the desires of your (my) heart. (I will) Commit your (my) way to the Lord. (I will) Trust also in Him and He will do it. And He will bring forth (my) your righteousness as the light and (my) your judgment as the noonday." *Psalm 37:3-6*

IN THE WORD

Let's look and see why the gates and walls around a city were so important in the Bible.

Please read Nehemiah 1 and 2. Both chapters in their entirety will explain why gates and walls were so important to Jerusalem.

The walls around Jerusalem were broken down, and the gates were burned. When the walls were destroyed, the people no longer had protection from intruders. Therefore, many of the people in Jerusalem were taken into captivity. The remnant who survived the captivity were in great distress because they were exposed and vulnerable.

Nehemiah began fasting and praying night and day before God, because the place where his descendants dwelled had been laid desolate. I like the fact that Nehemiah was very determined to seek God's face on behalf of his people. He confessed the sins of the sons of Israel to God. He knew that his people had acted corruptly against God and had not kept His commandments, and that is why God allowed the gates and walls around Jerusalem to be destroyed.

Why were the gates and walls so significant to Jerusalem? The city of Jerusalem was surrounded by walls—this meant protection for the inhabitants of the city. The walls were huge. Some scholars say that the stones used to build these walls measured up to thirty feet long, eight feet wide, four feet high, and weighed over eighty tons.

The gates were also very significant to the city. When they closed at night, no one came in or went out. During the day, the gates were open. People would gather for bargaining, conversations, news, and legal business at the gates. Different items would be sold at each gate within the city, which would, therefore, give a particular gate its name. You can read more about the gates in Nehemiah 3. They were the weakest points in the city's walls, therefore, they were the focal point of an enemy's attack. Once the enemy broke through a gate, they could possess the city. The remnant of Jerusalem did not have gates and walls for protection—they now had to protect themselves.

When you experience hurtful events, your gates have been burned and the walls of protection have tumbled down around you. So you begin to build your own walls of self-protection. Your walls are built with layers upon layers of impenetrable steel. Your gates are so heavy that they are rarely opened, so there is no need for conversation, bargaining, or any interaction. The city within you has become barren and desolate. You see no need to let anyone enter. Beloved, these are not the walls that God wants surrounding your city. God wants to build His walls of protection around you, but you must be willing to let Him.

Let's go back to Nehemiah 2. Nehemiah was the king's cup bearer. He was to taste the wine before the king drank it to verify it was not poisoned. In those days, no one was supposed to be sad before the king, but Nehemiah's heart was so broken for his people that he could not help but be sad. The king noticed his appearance and asked why his heart was so sad. Nehemiah confessed his sadness to the king and requested that if he had found favor in the eyes of the king that he be sent to rebuild the walls of Jerusalem. The king granted him his request. Nehemiah found favor in the king's eyes. Do you believe that your heavenly king wants you to come before Him and confess your sadness? I do! You are important to Him!

Please write Matthew 7:11:

_____
_____
_____
_____

You're heavenly Father loves you and wants what is best for you!

Write down times when your gates have been burned, your walls knocked down, and your inner city ravaged:

_____
_____

_____

_____

_____

Now is the time to tear down those walls of self-protection and allow God to build His walls around you. You may have people mocking you and telling you it's useless—that you should give up. That is the way they treated Nehemiah. But if God is for you, who can be against you! Carry on! Your success depends on God, not people.

God wants to rebuild your walls that the enemy has torn down. Do you know what happens when you allow God to rebuild your walls? Once His walls are in place, you can work on rebuilding the city within. As you are rebuilding, at night when you sleep, God will close the gates for you. With the dawn of a new morning, it will be time to rise and shine to begin another day of rebuilding. Your gates will be open for trade, conversations, and business transactions. What once was a barren wasteland will begin to be revived and rejuvenated.

Please write Psalm 100:4-5:

_____

_____

_____

While rebuilding your inner city, you will reach points of frustration. You may feel like you have run out of resources, encounter an obstacle that is not easily moved, or get aggravated at someone trying to help you rebuild. In any event, the restoration of your inner city will not happen overnight. While rebuilding, you must deal with God directly on your issues. Sure, you can talk with a counselor, a friend, a pastor, or your spouse, but the one who knows you best is the one who created you. "For Thou didst form my inward parts; Thou didst weave me in my mother's womb" *(Ps. 139:13)*.

Don't run away from God. Run to him. God is big enough for you to run to in times of trouble. When you struggle, cry out to God and ask Him to show you His truth. God has a plan for your life. You simply must trust that He knows what's best.

While you are rebuilding, build a trusting relationship with God too. Trust brings about restoration. How do you begin to develop a trusting relationship with God, your Father?

Please read Matthew 6:25-34.

Three times it tells you "do not be anxious" (verses 25, 31, and 34). Are you more important to God than a bird? Do you ever see a bird on a tree limb pacing back and forth, worried if he will find food for the day? No! The bird flies, and God instinctively steers him to the food. Do you see birds arguing with each other about who is going to get the next twig for the nest? No! They build the nest until it's completed. You are more important than a bird. Do you know why?

Please write 1 Corinthians 8:6:

_____

_____

_____

YOU EXIST FOR HIM! God created you for fellowship. God, the creator of the universe, wants to fellowship with YOU! How awesome is that?! God loves you and desires to give you His best. Learn to receive the gifts that God has for you. In receiving God's perfect gifts, you will learn to trust Him.

Hang in there!

PRAYER TIME

Father, thank you for giving me the desire to seek out friendships from other people. Thank you for surrounding me with people who I can reach out to and love and those who will return that love. Thank you, Lord, that I don't have to go through life alone, even though I may be single or feel single in a relationship. You have blessed me with a family and with friends to do life with, and I am so grateful! Lord, sometimes I have a hard time trusting people, because of past hurts. Thank you for giving me a spirit of discernment that I may be able to see past the superficial mask each person presents and help me love them the way You do. Thank you for laughter and putting people in my life to not only laugh with, but cry with as well. Thank you for loving others through me, and may I be a gateway to show others the ultimate love of Your Son, Jesus, who died on the cross for me because He loved me so much. In the name of Jesus, Amen.

it matters ...
That You Reach Out

Years ago, I experienced a time in my Christian walk when I felt like God could never love someone like me. As a teenager, I had been such a bad girl, and there was just no way that God could fully forgive and love me. I thought this constantly. Then a friend invited me to a Walk to Emmaus weekend, which I had never attended. This once in a lifetime spiritual retreat is supposed to transform your Christian walk. You know me—always up for a great adventure. I went. As a matter of fact, this event occurred just after I had gone through the year of forgiveness, when God had me seeking forgiveness from anyone and everyone I had done wrong. So I felt like this retreat was good timing—I needed a break.

My friend took me to the Walk on a Thursday evening. I didn't know anyone there, but that was okay, because I was not a wimp. I registered and then checked my bags into a room. My friend and I walked back to the registration area, and she introduced me to several people who would be at the Walk for the entire retreat, which would end on Sunday. Then we all spent some time worshipping Jesus. As the evening concluded, my friend said goodbye and left. She would pick me up at the end of the retreat.

The only people in the room were the participants and some of the workers for the weekend. We were asked to remove any watches and pack up any electronic devices in our luggage and not remove them until the weekend ended. They further elaborated that this weekend was not about time, but it would be focused solely on the Lord. I liked that! My kind of weekend! I was all about getting rid of earthly distractions. My daughter was with my parents, so I wasn't worried about her. Finally, they asked us to remain silent from that moment on until breakfast the next day. They further elaborated that they would have a special way of waking us up each day.

I'm into being obedient, so I remained silent, but I wanted to know how they were going to wake us up. I'm very nosey, but did not say anything. I headed back to my room, and once inside it, I noticed my roommate had checked in and left her bags on her bed. A few moments later, she walked through the door. I had never seen her before. Due to the no-talking thing, we nodded at each other, pointed at our name cards on our lapels, then got ready for bed. Tell me, how weird is that—sleeping in the same room with someone you don't know at all and can't speak to? Oh well, I just hoped she was a sincere

Christian and wouldn't kill me in my sleep or anything like that. Yes, I had major trust issues too.

The suspense of finding out how we were going to be awakened the next day came all too soon, as I felt like I had just closed my eyes when I heard the ringing of a bell outside my door along with a loud knock. I popped up out of bed and ran to answer the door, but the knocker/ringer person had moved on to the next door. We were still in silence mode. I pointed to the bathroom, and my roommate shook her head no, so I got a quick bath and dried my hair when, suddenly, we heard the bell again. It was breakfast time, so no makeup. We headed to the cafeteria, where we were greeting by people singing. *Okay, I haven't had my coffee yet, and this is a little much this early in the morning*, I thought. Being a good little Christian girl, I didn't say anything. I just smiled and someone pointed toward the coffee. I must have had that "I need caffeine" look on my face.

Finally, not long after, we were allowed to talk. After breakfast, we took turns introducing ourselves to each other. The Walk director explained several events that would take place throughout the weekend and asked us to have an attitude of surrender. We all freshened up before the first meeting started. As we walked out of the cafeteria, a whole group of people came in and began cleaning up behind us. Wow! That was very nice! I never had anyone picking up after me. Back in our room, we found that our beds had been made, and on our pillows we found cute little handmade crosses. How nice! I liked this Walk stuff!

We arrived in the conference room for our first meeting. I won't go into a lot of detail, because I don't want to spoil the weekend for someone who has never before attended a Walk. As the days rolled along, we spent time with God, we sang, we experienced a time of forgiveness, and we were served and loved on. I have never experienced anything like it. Throughout that weekend, God loved me through other people—people I did not know. People reached out to me, hugged me, ministered to me, and we laughed together and cried together. When Sunday came around, the wall of self-protection I had hidden behind for so long had cracked. I could receive the love these people were showing me. For the first time since I had become a Christian, I felt like God loved me. It was very overwhelming, and it was a lovely experience. If you've never been to a Walk to Emmaus retreat, I highly recommend attending.

During the week following the retreat, a lot of things sank in and I began to care about myself. When you know God loves you, you have a different attitude toward yourself. As a teenager, I was kind of wild and had been sexually promiscuous. Through the years, I realized the negative impact of those bad choices. I also realized that I loved God so much that I wanted to commit the rest of my life to Him, serve Him, and love Him. It was then that I spoke out loud my commitment to God, and I expressed that my desire was to serve Him and honor Him, which meant that I would never have another sexual relationship outside of marriage.

I committed my whole life to Him, right then and there. It felt good! I broke up with the guy I had been dating—of course we had been involved in a sexual relationship. He had a hard time believing I was breaking up with him because of God, but I did. A peace descended over me in making this decision, and

I knew that God would see me through this phase of sexual abstinence, however long it ended up being. It lasted for eleven years, five months, two weeks, four days, fifteen hours, twenty minutes, and thirty-seven seconds until I got married. Ha! All in all, it was around eleven and a half years before I married, and during this time God helped me maintain my commitment of sexual abstinence. Yes, it was hard, but worth it.

A few months after I made this commitment to God, I was asleep one night and God gave me a dream. In it, I stood in an auditorium before a group of kids. I was speaking with them about pro-life and abstinence issues. When I awoke, I prayed and asked God if this was something already in place or if I needed to start it myself. I went to work and shared the dream with my boss, who was also a Christian. He had no idea where to start, but suggested I talk with his wife. He said she was always involved in different ministries and would probably give me a good starting point, if nothing else.

I called my boss's wife, and we planned a lunch date for the next week. During lunch, she asked why I thought God wanted me to get involved in this type of ministry. I opened up and shared that I'd had an abortion at the age of eighteen. Until this point, I had not shared that part of my life with anyone and would have been totally afraid to share it with her, but I could see how much she loved the Lord and loved others. I knew my secret would be safe with her. I was right. She had so much compassion and reached out to me in love, when I shared my life with her. I also shared with her about the commitment I made to remain sexually abstinent until marriage. She suggested that I speak with the people at a local crisis pregnancy center

(CPC). She was not sure what type of ministries they offered, but thought it would be a good starting point.

I got back to the office, looked up the number for the CPC, and gave them a call. I spoke with the director and made an appointment to meet with her later in the week. When the day arrived, the receptionist ushered me to the director's office, and soon the director wanted to know why I wanted to get involved with their CPC. Once again, I allowed myself to be vulnerable. I told the director that I had had an abortion. I didn't mention the dream I'd had, however, because I didn't want her to think I was weird.

After I finished talking, the director informed me about three areas of ministry I could get involved with at their center: 1) I could counsel women who were contemplating having an abortion, 2) I could minister to women who'd already had an abortion, or 3) I could go into the public school system and share a message of sexual abstinence with the kids. I almost jumped out of the chair. This was it! I really wanted to get involved in this program. The end of the school year was close, so I signed up to attend their summer training classes.

After the training had ended and the new school year had begun, I was nervous to start the program—I'm actually a very shy person. I received my assignment, gathered my supplies, and headed to the school. Finally there, each step I took in the hallway toward the appointed classroom felt awkward. I just knew I would freeze and not complete the presentation. Suddenly, a little sixth grade boy came up to me and asked, "Are you going to be our speaker today?" I smiled and nodded yes. He further questioned, with an excited look, "Are you going to be speaking to us about penises and vaginas?" God knew exactly what I needed to break the ice that day and that did it! I was good to go. The abstinence presentations were my new favorite thing to do. All the kids hear in school is, "Here's a condom, learn how to use it." I loved educating the kids about the emotional and physical consequences associated with having sex outside of marriage.

It matters that you make a positive
difference in the lives of others.

I had been volunteering with the abstinence program for about six months when God opened the doors for me to attend an abortion recovery program at an affiliated CPC. God healed my heart in an amazing way through this ministry. About two weeks after I had completed the program, I was approached by the CPC I had been involved with, to become the director of the abortion recovery ministry. I prayed about it and felt like God was giving me the go-ahead to switch careers.

Several months later, I began my in-state missionary journey with this CPC. It was an exciting time, and I was thrilled to be part of this great adventure. I had been on staff with this CPC for about a month when I learned that another CPC across town had closed its doors several years ago because there was no one to run it. I thought of all the young ladies in the area who might need help and direction in the event of an unplanned pregnancy, and I knew that center needed to reopen. Our goal was to steer them clear of an abortion clinic. I approached our organization's powers that be and asked if we could all pray about me reopening the CPC, in addition to continuing to lead the abortion recovery ministry at the current location. We spent a couple of weeks in prayer over the request. Then we decided to reopen the CPC.

I checked out the old CPC building across town, a bank-owned home located in a commercial district. I pulled up to find a little yellow house, probably built in the forties, with a covered front porch. In my mind's eye, I could see a happy couple sitting on rocking chairs there and waving as neighbors drove by, but then time passed and the area went commercial—except for this little house. My reverie over, I opened the door and walked in to find a receptionist desk. To the left was a living room complete with couch, chairs, tables, lamp, and a fireplace with a wooden cover. To the right was the entrance to the kitchen, which had been turned into an office/breakroom. Straight ahead from the front door was a hall, and behind the first door on the right was a full-size bathroom complete with a tub. There were two bedrooms, one on either side of the hall that had been converted into counseling rooms. Each room had a couple of comfortable chairs, table, and a lamp. At the end of the hall a door led down to a half-basement.

I saw great potential in this house. However, it had a *smell* throughout. I attributed this to the age of the home and the fact that it had been vacant for several years. I didn't really give it another thought.

Later, one of my closest friends and I cleaned up the house to prepare it for its reopening. After cleaning all day, we were exhausted. We had talked about all the possibilities of this ministry opportunity, how to promote its existence, and all the fundraisers we could do. We decided the half-basement would be a great place to establish an infant clothes closet. I was so excited! My friend had to leave for the day, so I was there finishing up. Finally, as I was gathering everything to leave, I looked around to see if there was anything we had missed. As I did so, I noticed the *smell* was still there—not as strong as before, but still . . .

I was really surprised. We had done a good and thorough job cleaning. We had also discussed the *smell* when we arrived, and we had agreed it would be gone by the time we finished our work. God's Word says to pray about everything, so I usually do. So I prayed and asked God to show me the source of the smell. Suddenly, God directed my attention to the solid wooden cover over the fireplace in the living room. I walked over to the cover, pulled it back, and discovered a pile of dead squirrels.

Yep, that's the *smell*. I called one of the facility's directors and told him about the dead squirrels. I asked him what he was going to do about it. I'm a girl. Dealing with a fireplace full of dead squirrels is NOT my thing. He said he would try to get out there in a couple of weeks and get the squirrels out, but couldn't make any promises.

I was a little frustrated. We were planning to open the center in a couple of weeks, plus my friend and I had been cleaning all day. While the place smelled a little better than it had, that didn't compensate for the fact that those dead squirrels would be stinking up the place for yet another couple of weeks. I prayed to God to ask Him to provide someone to clean out the squirrels. As I finished my prayer, I so clearly remember God speaking to my heart and saying, "I called you, not to put you up on a pedestal, but to be My servant. Now, clean out the squirrels."

Just leave it to God to be equal opportunity about cleaning dead squirrels out of a fireplace. I recalled seeing a shovel in the basement, so I got the shovel and brought in the garbage can from outside and began the dirty deed. I shoveled out all the squirrels, along with a few chippy chipmunks, and set the garbage can out by the road for pickup to take the rodents to their final resting place at the garbage dump. Yuck! On the way home, I called my parents' house and told Dad about the squirrel adventure. He was quick to point out that the fireplace, obviously, was uncovered from the outside and needed to be covered to prevent future dead squirrel excavations. The next day, I met Dad at the center. He was equipped with his ladder, climbed up on the roof, and properly covered the chimney top. He came in and looked around to inspect the facility and discovered there was no hot water. He crawled up under the house and found a broken pipe. He repaired the pipe so we could have hot water. He's a great dad!

It matters that I'm a servant, instead of a pedestal topper.

I was involved in a ministry outreach through my church, which scheduled a weekend retreat. It would be a time of fellowship, a time of brainstorming for upcoming outreach events, and a time of drawing closer to the Lord. Prior to the retreat, we were each asked to prepare a short devotional associated with a word from the Bible. My assigned word was "servant." I prayed a lot about the word, because servant can mean different things to different people. As retreat weekend approached, I still wasn't sure what God wanted me to share. He hadn't put any words in my heart, so I kept praying. The first day of the retreat weekend arrived—still nothing. I was grateful to learn that I was to be the last one to share on Sunday afternoon right before the retreat ended, so I would have time to hear from God about what He wanted me to say. I've said before that it's always so important to be obedient to God and His leading, but I wasn't getting even an inkling of how I needed to be obedient in this situation. Throughout the weekend, different people asked me what I was going to share. I told them it would be a surprise. Well, it was going to be a surprise to me too.

Suddenly, after our Sunday morning message was over and while we were eating lunch, God gave me the message. After lunch, I got one of the big bowls that had previously held a couple of bags of chips, washed it, and half-filled it with water. I went to my room, got a towel, and took both my items to our meeting room. I asked the retreat leader to have everyone bring their chairs and put them in a semicircle in front of the room. She had every one rearrange their chairs, and she announced that I would be sharing what it means to be a servant. I did not utter a word, but I took my bowl and towel and knelt at the feet of the first person in line, removed their socks and shoes, then began to wash their feet. After I washed each foot, I dried it with the towel. I then moved to the next person and continued until every foot in that building was washed. Not a word was spoken, but there was not a dry eye in the place. We all knew what was required of us as we left the retreat that weekend. We were to be His servants. "If I then, the Lord and the Teacher, washed your feet, you also ought to wash one another's feet" *(John 13:14).*

It matters that we are His servants—

the hands and feet of Jesus.

POSITIVE WORD CONFESSIONS

"Beloved, let us (me) love one another, for love is from God; and everyone who loves is born of God and knows God." *1 John 4:7*

"And so, as those who (I) have been chosen of God, holy and beloved, (I will) put on a heart of compassion, kindness, humility, gentleness and patience; bearing with one another, and forgiving each other, whoever has a complaint against anyone; just as the Lord forgave you (me), so also should you (I)." *Colossians 3:12-13*

IN THE WORD

PURITY

"And everyone who has this hope fixed on Him purifies himself, just as He is pure" *(1 John 3:3).*

To be pure means to make clean, to sanctify, set apart. God wants you to be pure in the way you think and the way you live. "Purity" was a big word in my life, because I had not lived a life of purity. My life was quite the opposite when I was a teenager. Then at the age of twenty-five, I became a Christian and all of my old, impure ways of living came back to haunt me. After I became a Christian, a friend shared with me how important it was for him to live a life of purity (sexual abstinence) until he got married. He said it was the greatest gift he could ever give his wife. Wow! No one had ever shared anything like that with me.

I began praying about purity, and God gave me a vision of a piece of pie. He said, "Before you have sex with someone, your heart is like this whole piece of pie and once you have a sexual relationship with someone and that relationship breaks up, it's as if you have cut a piece of pie and given it to that other person. If you have another sexual relationship and that relationship breaks up, another piece of your pie is then given away." As odd as this vision was, it made sense to me for two reasons: 1) I really like most any kind of pie and don't really care to share my pie with anyone, and 2) I could see there was a permanent difference in the pie after the pieces were gone.

Eventually, I made the commitment to God that I would remain sexually abstinent until marriage. Therefore, eleven and a half years later on my wedding day, my husband and I had sex. I will say that it felt really good to freely give myself to my husband. We were in a committed marriage relationship, and that is the way God designed a sexual relationship to take place.

Beloved, if you are single, I encourage you to maintain a life of sexual purity until marriage. You may ask, "How far is too far?" My reply, "Take your question before the Lord, and let Him reveal his plan for your life."

Please look up each Scripture to better understand the meaning of purity:

Psalm 24:3-4

Psalm 51:10

Matthew 5:8

Philippians 4:8

1 Timothy 1:5

2 Timothy 2:22

Titus 1:15-16
Hebrews 10:22
James 1:27
James 3:17

Please describe what purity means to you and what changes you need to make to keep your heart from being defiled:

_____

_____

_____

_____

_____

_____

SANCTIFICATION

"Husbands, love your wives just as Christ also loved the church and gave Himself up for her; that He might sanctify her, having cleansed her by the washing of water with the word." *Ephesians 5:25-26*

Christ gave himself up for the church (His bride), that He might sanctify her. How was the church sanctified in this process?

Please read each Scripture to see how we are sanctified by the washing of water:

Acts 22:16
1 Corinthians 6:11
Titus 3:4-7

Please read each Scripture to see how we are sanctified by the Word:

John 15:3
John 17:17-21

Please write 1 Peter 3:15-16:

_____

_____

_____

_____

You are called to sanctify Christ as Lord in your heart. You should always be willing to share Christ's love with others. The more you realize His presence within you, the more like Him you want to become.

Please read 1 Thessalonians 4:3-8.

It is the will of God that you live in a state of sanctification. This involves self-control, a fruit of the Spirit. Self-control is restraint exercised over one's own impulses, emotions, and desires. When your feelings of desire get out of hand, you must hold back: self-control.

It is so important to know what God's Word says about such things as sexual immorality, so you can live your life accordingly. There are so many study helps and commentaries that you can use to obtain a clearer understanding of God's Word.

"Jesus said to him, 'I am the way, and the truth, and the life; no one comes to the Father, but through me'" *(John 14:6)*.

When you accept Jesus, you accept:

His Way—accept His ways

His Truth—conform your life to the truths of His Word

His Life—change your life and no longer live for the lusts of the flesh

God will help you with the sanctification process:

He will convict you of sin.

He will help you repent and turn away from sin.

He will forgive you of sin.

He will cleanse you from sin.

He will give you power over sin.

Sanctification does not happen overnight. It is a growth process. God will constantly grow you up in Him. Step by step. Day by day. When you go to God in prayer, read God's Word, apply God's Word to your everyday life, trust God, and humble yourself before Him, you will be amazed at the good changes that will occur.

HOPE

Hope is the expectation of future good. If you have no hope, you waste away in despair. Life events can get in the way of hope. If you keep your eyes focused on Jesus and allow Him to walk with you through the valleys of life, you will always be able to experience hope.

I want to share with you one hope you can be confident in—the return of your Lord and Savior Jesus Christ! If you put your hope in Jesus, your worldly hopes will pale in comparison to the hope you have in Jesus!

Please read the following Scriptures regarding hope:

Psalm 9:18
Psalm 38:15
Psalm 71:5
Romans 5:3-8
Romans 12:10-13
Romans 15:13
Galatians 5:5
Ephesians 1:18
Colossians 1:23
Colossians 1:27
1 Thessalonians 5:8
Titus 3:7
1 Peter 3:15

Have hope and confidence in God, Jesus, and the Holy Spirit. They will never let you down. You will not be alone when your hope is in the Lord. He is your Good Shepherd, and He is constantly watching out for you. He will come searching for you, if you go astray.

PRAYER TIME

Holy Father, thank you for being the Lord of my life. Thank you for the valleys You've carried me through. Thank you for the people You bring into my life to encourage me along the way. Thank you for being the lifter of my head. I love You, and Lord I ask that You show me how to love others. I want to love them the way You love them, and I want to serve them.

Please give me eyes to see those who are hurt and broken from bad experiences. Help me look for the good in everything. Your Word says, "And we know that God causes all things to work together for good to those who love God, to those who are called according to His purpose" *(Rom. 8:28)*. I know I am called, so please help me discover my purpose here on earth. Help me to seek Your face. Thank you for giving me a hunger and thirst for You and Your Word. Thank you for opening doors of opportunity for ministry and to serve others, but help me not forget that the greatest ministry is where I may be currently located. Please help me be mindful that my life is a witness to others. My attitude and my actions need to line up with Your Word. If they do not, please help me see how I can remove any bad roots from my life, so I may give You glory in everything I say and everything I do. In the name of Jesus, Amen.

it matters ...
Staying Close to Family

I have mentioned my family throughout this book. Now, I want to share a few stories that show why my family is so important. I offer the following:

As a youngster, I was the most awkwardly shy person you would ever meet. I never warmed up to strangers. For example, when I started first grade, Mom let me out of the car at school and I stood there crying for two solid weeks as I watched her drive away. Come to find out years later, she cried as she watched me from the rearview mirror. I was the oldest of four siblings, so I had to break her in. At home I was not so shy and played with neighborhood friends. As a matter of fact, all the neighborhood kids hung out at my house. My parents had made it inviting. They were always a lot of fun and were very involved in our lives. You might think I'm kidding, but neighborhood kids would be sitting at our kitchen table at six on a Saturday morning to find out what my parents had planned for the day. We never locked our doors! Mom would treat everyone to a homemade waffle slathered with peanut butter and Aunt Jemima syrup. Yummy! Then we all started our great adventure for the day, whatever that happened to be.

Dad was always the policeman as we were all riding our skateboards and Big Wheels in the basement and on the driveway. Dad always kept spare Big Wheel tires on hand because we were constantly wearing them out. We all had motocross bicycles and made trails through the woods. Dad would quarterback for both football teams, when we played football in the front yard. Believe it or not, hauling a load of trash to the dump was an adventure. I can't count the number of times we had weenie roasts in the backyard, made gallons of homemade ice cream, and grilled, grilled, and grilled again. We would pitch tents in the backyard and camp. Anything we could get into, we did.

When I was ten, Mom wanted me to become a cheerleader. She thought it would help me overcome my shyness. I became a cheerleader and my oldest brother became a football player. About the third week of cheerleading practice, I came home and told Mom that I did not like cheerleading and was not planning to go back to practice anymore. Mom made the most profound statement, which I carry with me to this day. "Young lady," she said, "you made a commitment to be a cheerleader, and it doesn't matter if you like it or not. You are going to carry out your commitment and finish this year of cheering." I kept on cheering and finally began to enjoy it.

We put in a lot of grueling hours to prepare for the Cheerleading Championship Tournament, where we would cheer against numerous other teams. At the tournament, our team cheered its heart out. Mom watched from the arena stands, and our team took home the first place trophy. Mom was so proud, and so was I. After football season ended that year, I decided that I couldn't do better than first place, so the next year I became the Gatorade Girl for my brother's football team. I was happy!

It matters that you give your all to any commitment you make and finish well.

Mom is an excellent seamstress. She can make anything by hand. As we became more involved in the football world, Mom began making cheerleader uniforms each year. She was inundated with orders, so she'd put all of us kids to work in her sewing area in the basement. We had an assembly line going with each of us performing a different task in making uniforms, but Mom did the hard part. We were just her assistants.

I wanted to be like Mom, so when Granny gave us a box of material scraps, I thought it would be fun to make a quilt. Mom showed me how to cut out the pieces of material into the same size squares, and she showed me how to use the sewing machine to sew the patchwork pieces. Once I got them all sewn together for the top part, we added a bottom layer, filled it with cotton, put it on the quilting frame, and began quilting it. It took a long time to finish, but we finished it together. Actually, Mom did a lot more quilting than I did. It's probably one of the ugliest quilts I have ever seen, but my brother loved it and kept it until it fell apart.

In later years, Mom started crocheting and made a beautiful blanket for my king-sized bed. I wouldn't take a million dollars for it. Just recently, Mom decided she wanted to make a quilt for each of her kids and grandkids to remember her by. I wish I could share a picture with you of the quilt she made for me. It's absolutely gorgeous, all handmade, and perfectly sewn. In the top left corner of the quilt, she wrote a note:

For Amy,
I hope you will always remember my love for you! Stay warm!
Love, Mama

Priceless!

It matters that we keep things that
remind us of special people in our lives.

My parents loved to travel. Travel can mean different things to different people, but my parents' version of traveling meant going to the beach for a long weekend, heading to the mountains, driving out into the country to find a spot for a picnic and a creek to splash around in, finding covered bridges, camping at a local state park, or visiting family. It really did not matter where we went, just as long as we were going somewhere together.

My parents are very special for, among other reasons, always lending a helping hand to others. It did not matter who it was, where it was, or how they helped them—they always helped people. I can't tell you how many times we would be driving back home from a beach trip and Dad would see a couple of Navy guys hitchhiking home. He would pick them up, and off we would go. We always had a big station wagon, so we all moved to the back and made room to accommodate our wonderful military men. Also, Dad was very mechanically inclined and always had a toolbox on hand, so when he would see someone in a broken-down car, he always stopped to help them and usually got their car running.

Through the years, my parents took a couple of kids into our home temporarily, because they didn't have anyone to love them. We all just moved around to make room. My parents were full of love and always shared everything. Sick relatives lived with us at different times. Mom nursed them back to health with her good cooking and care, then sent them on their way. Everything was always a family effort—keeping the house clean, keeping the yard picked up and mowed, cleaning up after dinner each night. Mom always cooked a nice dinner, and we all sat around the table to eat and share stories about our day. We would have family time in the living room, where my parents would play their favorite albums, and we would sit around and enjoy the music. No one kid was ever more special than the other, and we all pitched in to help. My parents taught all of us how to give and how to love others, and all four of us are very good about extending love and kindness to other people, as we have grown into our own ways of loving and giving. I'm so grateful for my parents.

It matters that parents teach their children how to be good givers.

On one of our family's great adventures, we were headed to the lake. On the way, we passed by a water works facility. In front of it flowed two large ponds, separated by a manmade walkway that housed the treatment machines. I was about twelve-years-old, and my parents were usually good about showing us new things, helping us to see how different things worked, and just always in training mode. Dad pointed out that our clean water came from the facility. I looked over at the ponds and asked him, "Which one of the ponds is hot, and which one is cold?" Did I mention that I'm a natural blonde? From the front seat, Dad shook his head. Immediately, I knew something was amiss. "Amy," he said, "do you know what the big round thing under the stairs in the basement is?" I responded, "Of course, it's a hot … oh."

I'm now grown, still blonde, and live at the very lake we visited that day. Each time my parents drive by that water works facility to see me, they laugh and ask, "Which one of those ponds is hot, and which one is cold?" Recently, I underwent a surgical procedure and needed someone to drive me home afterward. My parents are always my drivers, and this particular day was no exception. Of course, we passed by the water works facility on the way back to my house. Dad asked me if I ever figured out which one was hot and which one was cold. Ha-ha. Very funny.

Dad has shared that story with countless people through the years, and each time they pass by the facility they think of me and get a good laugh.

It matters that my life brings laughter to others.

POSITIVE WORD CONFESSIONS

"Let no unwholesome word proceed from your (my) mouth, but only such a word as is good for edification according to the need of the moment, that it may give grace to those to hear." *Ephesians 4:29*

"For I am confident of this very thing, that He who began a good work in you (me) will perfect it until the day of Christ Jesus." *Philippians 1:6*

IN THE WORD

RIGHTEOUSNESS
Please read Romans 6:12-16, and write verse 16:

_____

_____

_____

You are a slave to the one you obey. Do you want to be a slave of sin resulting in death?

_____

_____

Do you want to be a slave of obedience to God resulting in righteousness?

_____

_____

Please read Revelation 19:1-16, and look at what Jesus did for you as it relates to righteousness.

As Jesus's bride, how are you clothed in verse 8?

_____

_____

Can you put a price tag on this robe?

_____

_____

How is Jesus clothed in verse 13?

_____

_____

Your clothes have been purchased for a very high price. When God looks at you, He sees you through Jesus—through His blood. Therefore, when God looks at you, He sees you cleansed—white and clean. God sees you as righteous, through Jesus. Jesus wears a robe dipped in blood, so that you may be "clothed with fine linen, white and clean."

Please get a blanket, sheet, or towel. Wrap this around your shoulders; this is symbolic of your robe of righteousness. Please read Isaiah 61:10 and answer the following questions:

What type of garment are you clothed with?

_____

_____

What type robe have you been wrapped with?

_____

How does it feel to be clothed with such fine linen and to be treated with such worth and dignity?

_____

_____

_____

To be clothed with garments of salvation and a robe of righteousness is above and beyond any blessing you could ever hope for. You are so special, because Jesus loves you!

Write a prayer of praise and adoration to your God in heaven who sits on the throne. He allowed His Son's blood to be shed so that you might become the righteousness of God in Christ Jesus!

_____

_____

_____

_____

_____

_____

HOLINESS

Please write 1 Peter 1:14-16:

_____

_____

_____

_____

Holiness means to be sacred, to be set apart.

Please read Hebrews 12:10, and answer the following question:

What does God want you to share in?

_____

_____

Please read 2 Peter 1:3-8, and list the seven ways God wants you to live found in verses 5-7:

1.

2.

3.

4.

5.

6.

7.

God wants you to live a life of excellence and have knowledge and apply self-control. He wants you to persevere, live a life of godliness, express brotherly kindness to your neighbor, and love people.

Please read 2 Peter 3:8-13, and list the two ways God wants you to live found in verse 11:

1.

2.

God wants you to live with a conduct of holiness and godliness. The times are short, and you never know when your last day will be on this earth. God wants you to make wise choices, and live for Him every day.

Please read 2 Corinthians 7:1.

God does not want you to live in sin. He wants you to cleanse yourself from all defilement of the world. Let's look at the verses prior to this verse and see how God wants you to live:

Please read 2 Corinthians 6:14-18, and complete the following statements:

Verse 14 – Do not be bound together with _____

Verse 16 – We are the temple of _____

Verse 17 – Come out from their midst and be _____

God wants you to go into the world to share the love of Jesus, but He does not want you to be a part of the world.

Please read out loud 1 Thessalonians 3:12-13 as a prayer.

That's what God wants for you—a heart unblameable in holiness before God. How can you accomplish this state of holiness?

WALK IN LOVE!

PRAYER TIME

Precious Lord, thank you for surrounding me with a loving family. Not everyone has a loving family, so I ask that You surround people I know with someone to love them well. Someone who will show them how to give and love others well. Please give me eyes to see those who might be hurting, those who need a helping hand, those who are at the end of their rope. Give me the desire to take dinner to a friend who has just gone through surgery or take a pot of soup to someone who might be sick. Please give me the will to carry my neighbor to the finish line in life, when they have fallen and don't have the will or ability to get up on their own. Lord, I don't want to be an enabler, I want to be a helper—Your helper. I want to show others the way to find true, everlasting love and that is through Jesus. Thank you for opening the doors of heaven and pouring out your blessings on me, so I can go and bless others. In the name of Jesus, Amen.

it matters ...

Grandkids

Have I mentioned that I have two grandkids who I absolutely adore with all my heart?! They are Nanny's little sweethearts. At the time of this writing, my granddaughter is ten-years-old and my grandson is eight. I offer the following funny stories:

My granddaughter got a four-wheeler when she was six. She loved riding it around my house. One day, I finally got her to stop long enough, so we could build a fire in the fire pit out by the lake and roast some weenies for dinner. The next morning as I was sitting on my deck drinking a cup of coffee, she came out to join me before getting on her four-wheeler. I mentioned to her that she had left her helmet on the swing and that it probably had some dew on it that she would need to wipe off. She went out to the swing, got her helmet, and as she began to ascend the stairs to the deck, she said, "Thank goodness, Nanny. Look, there's no doo doo on my helmet."

One day I was taking my grandkids for an outing. They were camped out in the backseat of my car. I don't know what prompted my granddaughter to ask this question, but she said, "Nanny, what's under the seat?" I thought it was a trick question, so I responded with a question, "Monsters?" Apparently that was the wrong answer, because as I looked in my rearview mirror, they both had horrified looks, their feet were in the seat, and they were looking down at the bottom of it. As any loving grandmother would do, I started laughing. I could not stop laughing, but I did manage to tell them I was just playing. Of course, I got scolded for the bad answer. Finally, after I quit laughing, my granddaughter asked again, "Really, Nanny, what's under the seat?" I responded, "Carpet." Then I added, "A pen and maybe a couple of stale French fries too." I couldn't stop laughing. Am I an evil grandmother?

One day, I was keeping my granddaughter, so her mom could run to the grocery store. My granddaughter asked to borrow my phone so she could contact her mom. She wanted to remind her to pick up whipped cream for her strawberries. Here are the text messages they traded:

Emma: Get some wipe cream. (2:23 p.m.)

Mom: I'm sorry, are you having booty issues? Do you need to feel more clean down there? (2:25 p.m.)

Emma: No. I just want some wipe cream. (2:26 p.m.)

Mom: Whipped cream … not wipe cream. (2:27 p.m.)

Emma: SORRY (2:28 p.m.)

BTW it's me Emma (2:29 p.m.)
Helloooooooooooooooooooo (2:30 p.m.)
Amy: Too funny!! It's Amy now. (2:58 p.m.)

Shortly after I sent the last text, my daughter walked in the door with the whipped cream, laughing hysterically. She said, "I knew something was wrong when you didn't come back with an LOL after I corrected you about the spelling. I knew SORRY wasn't you." Wipe cream, whipped cream—what's the difference. LOL!

Emma was in first grade and she was sick one day, so I had the privilege of escorting her to the doctor's office. In the waiting room, a couple of teenage girls sat next to us. Come to find out through our conversation, they were sisters and the big sister had brought her little sister to see the doctor. How nice! They got called back, then it happened—I got the Stranger Danger lecture.

It matters that my grandkids make me laugh—all the time!

I'm a grandkid too, who very much loved her maternal grandmother. Granny was the greatest grandmother in the world. She did not have a lot of possessions, but she showered a great deal of love on her grandchildren whenever she could. She lived in another city far enough away that when she visited, she would stay for several days. We loved to play the card game Shanghai Rummy. We would all play until we couldn't keep our eyes open at night. I loved being around her.

When I spent the night at Granny's house, I slept in the room that didn't get a lot of heat in the winter. She kept an electric blanket on the bed that kept me toasty warm. For some reason, she would wake up at four thirty every morning and when I smelled fried chicken and biscuits cooking, I woke up too. Granny made cowboy coffee. It was so strong it would make a woman grow face hair. Granny always used cute little teacups with a saucer for her coffee. She would pour us a cup, and we'd put four teaspoons full of sugar in it, plus milk, and we would sit and chat about everything and nothing at all. After breakfast, we would watch TV during the winter, but during the summer we would harvest the garden.

In the summer, Granny always had a fresh vegetable garden full of tomatoes, corn, hot peppers, mild peppers, okra, green beans, field peas, butter beans, and cucumbers. We would sit and shell peas, snap green beans, and talk, talk, talk. If there was ever anyone on the face of this earth who made me feel completely and totally loved, it was Granny. She never spoke a harsh word and was always so kind and loving. She took up crocheting in her spare time and made me this huge blanket with brown, orange, yellow, and cream stripes. Most people wouldn't appreciate it, but I wouldn't trade it for a million dollars, because Granny made it just for me. Today at my home, I have a sunroom that stays pretty chilly during the cold winter months. On the full-sized bed in that room, there are several blankets, along with the blanket that Granny made for me. Sometimes when it's really cold outside, I'll go sleep on that bed and think about Granny.

Years passed, and Granny began to be forgetful. We found out she had Alzheimer's disease. Granny would spend about three weeks with Mom, then spend three weeks with my uncle, and this went on for a few years until my mom's health was not doing well and my uncle was struggling to keep up with Granny. One day we were sitting on my parents' front porch, which faced a big pasture with cows across the street. Suddenly, Granny sat up straight, looked out at the pasture, and shouted at her two brothers, whom she called by name. "Get out of that river and quit drinking that beer," she told them. They had been deceased more than fifteen years.

Granny had always been a God-fearing woman and didn't like any beer drinking going on—even when she had Alzheimer's disease.

As Granny's disease worsened, she became more childlike. When my nephew was about three years old, she would chase him around the house. She was probably at the little girl stage of the disease. Her actions scared my nephew to death. Mom and my uncle decided to put Granny in a nursing home. She seemed to like the place, though she did escape a few times to the nearby mall. Several times, she would open the nursing home's emergency exit door, then hide in a nearby room to watch all the commotion. Granny was very mischievous. Mom had to go give her a talking to, not that it really helped.

Granny had Alzheimer's disease for about ten years. The first half of this time was spent at home, the last half in the nursing home. Occasionally, I would visit her, and it was always so hard to walk into a room and see a woman you loved so much, but who didn't have a clue who you were. Usually, I would wheel her outside on the front porch of the nursing home or just sit her in front of the window of her room. She loved to look outside or be outside. I would stand there, stroke her hair, and talk to her, and the whole time silent tears would stream down my face.

This chapter just would not have been complete without sharing how God chose to bless me with a wonderful grandmother.

It matters that Granny loved me and I loved her.

POSITIVE WORD CONFESSIONS

"The Lord is my shepherd, I shall not want. He makes me lie down in green pastures; He leads me beside quiet waters. He restores my soul; He guides me in the paths of righteousness for His name's sake. Even though I walk through the valley of the shadow of death, I fear no evil; for Thou art with me; Thy rod and Thy staff they comfort me. Thou dost prepare a table before me in the presence of my enemies; Thou has anointed my head with oil; my cup overflows. Surely goodness and lovingkindness will follow me all the days of my life, and I will dwell in the house of the Lord forever." *Psalm 23*

"Make me know Thy ways, O Lord; Teach me Thy paths. Lead me in Thy truth and teach me, for Thou art the God of my salvation; for Thee I wait all the day." *Psalm 25:4-5*

IN THE WORD

One thing I know for certain is this: The devil does not want you to forget your past.

Please write Luke 9:62:

_____

_____

_____

_____

Satan knows that as long as he can torment you with your failures, mistakes, and bad decisions, he will keep you from being effective in the kingdom of God. You will constantly be looking back at what could have been, rather than moving forward in the new life that Christ has given you. When you have experienced abuse, it is hard to accept the grace, compassion, and lovingkindness that God so earnestly desires to give you, His child. You might call it stubbornness.

Please read Nehemiah 9:16-17, and answer the following questions:

How did the fathers act?

_____

_____

Why would they not listen to God's commandments?

_____

_____

_____

_____

The Israelites became stiff-necked or stubborn. They no longer wanted to conform to God's commandments. They wanted to live their way, do what they wanted, and did not want anyone interfering. People get so accustomed to a certain way of life and when change enters the picture, they resist changing. It is easier to stay enslaved to the chains and bonds of misery, because it is a familiar way of life. People grow accustomed to the bondage and see no need for freedom. Sometimes they don't even know they are enslaved to sin. We already looked at the ten commandments in the first chapter of this book. These are the commandments the Israelites refused to follow.

The first four commandments in the Old Testament are summed up in the New Testament as follows: "And you shall love the Lord your God with all your heart, and with all your soul, and with all your mind, and with all your strength" *(Mark 12:30)*.

The last six commandments in the Old Testament are summed up in the New Testament as follows: "You shall love your neighbor as yourself" *(Mark 12:31)*.

GOD IS LOVE! God was LOVE throughout the Old Testament and continues to be LOVE throughout the New Testament and in your life today!

What happens when you fail to obey God's commandments? It grieves God's heart. The Holy Spirit will convict you to a point of seeking God's forgiveness. As you go through this process, the devil will put thoughts in your mind such as: Why would God forgive someone like you? There's no way God will forgive that sin.

God does not categorize sin as big or small, but people sure do. Murder is just as big a sin to God as gossip! Please keep this in mind as you continue this study. I'm giving you tools to defeat the strongholds the enemy has over your life.

Please write 2 Corinthians 7:10:

_____

_____

_____

_____

_____

Does this Scripture verse seem to be written especially for you? Are you tired of death in your life? Repentance is doing a one-hundred-eighty degree turn and walking away. This Scripture says that when you do have a godly sorrow over sin and repent, you will have no regret. When you desire to have a godly sorrow over sin in your life, it does not mean that you can pray a blanket prayer and everything will be okay—this would be the easy way out. Your prayer of godly sorrow must include two important concepts—first, acknowledgment of specific sin, and second, agreement with God about the destructive power of that sin.

When the Israelites came out of Egypt, God led them via the long route, because He knew if His people saw war, they would be inclined to turn around and run back to Egypt (Exodus 13:17). Along God's route, they saw the parting of the Red Sea (Exodus 14:21), the sweetening of the bitter waters at Marah (Exodus 15:25), and the daily manna from heaven (Exodus 16:4). These sights all revealed the power and trustworthiness of God. The Israelites needed to learn this lesson before they could establish their nation. If you try to take the easy way out, you will be inclined to turn around and return to the miry clay from which you have been attempting to escape.

Why is it important to have a godly sorrow over sin?

_____

_____

_____

_____

_____

_____

Please read the following Scripture verses:

Psalm 13:2
Psalm 31:10
Psalm 32:3
Psalm 38:3

Please write Matthew 20:28:

_____

_____

_____

_____

Let's say someone has kidnapped you and they are holding you for ransom. Upon receipt of this ransom, the kidnappers will let you go. Satan has been holding you in bondage—he's basically kidnapped your soul (mind, will, and emotions). Jesus has already given his soul to pay your ransom, so your soul can no longer be held captive. This is the beauty of having a godly sorrow over sin in your life. It produces a repentance without regret. The great thing about this is that even though Jesus has paid your ransom, you do not owe Him anything in return. How could you ever pay God back for His Son's death on the cross? There's no way possible. You can simply accept the love God extends to you as his adoptive child, through Christ His Son.

We are going to take a journey back to the Old Testament to determine why Christ's death on the cross was so significant.

Please read Leviticus 16.

Once a year, Aaron would make a sacrifice for the Israelite's sin. He would take two goats—one would be slain and its blood sprinkled on the mercy seat to make atonement (to satisfy) for the people's sin; with the second goat, Aaron would lay both his hands on its head and confess over it all the iniquities and transgressions of the people regarding their sin. This second goat would be considered the scapegoat (goat of removal) and be carried away into a solitary land by a man who was fit and ready. This goat would then be released into the wilderness. The only way the people in the Old Testament could receive forgiveness of sin was by the shed blood of the sacrifice of the first goat and having their sins carried away into the wilderness to be remembered no more by the second goat.

Moving on to the New Testament.

Please write John 1:29:

_____

_____

_____

_____

Why do you think John the Baptist referred to Jesus as a lamb?

_____

_____

_____

Please write 1 Peter 1:18-19:

_____

_____

_____

_____

_____

_____

Jesus was your sacrifice—your lamb! Jesus's blood was shed on the cross at Calvary to cleanse you of sin. What exactly happened at Calvary?

Please read Romans 8:31-37.

As God's Son (Jesus, Lamb of God) hung on the cross, all your sins were placed on Him. "Now from the sixth hour darkness fell upon all the land until the ninth hour. And about the ninth hour Jesus cried out with a loud voice, saying, 'ELI, ELI, LAMA SABACHTHANI?' that is, 'My God, My God, why hast Thou forsaken me?' " *(Matt. 27:45-46)* At this point, Jesus was separated (to go away, depart) from His Father. Your sin separated Jesus from God. Because Jesus has experienced this separation, you do not have to. Praise God!

Please read Romans 8:38-39, and list the ten things that CANNOT separate you from the love of God:

1.

2.

3.

4.

5.

6.

7.

8.

9.

10.

Nothing can separate you from God's love, because Jesus has already experienced this separation for you.

"And when He had taken some bread and given thanks, He broke it, and gave it to them, saying, 'This is My body which is given for you; do this in remembrance of Me.' And in the same way He took the cup after they had eaten, saying, 'This cup which is poured out for you is the new covenant in My blood' " *(Luke 22:19-20)*.

The separation from God was the brokenness that Jesus experienced for you. After the brokenness occurred, Jesus gave up his spirit. "But one of the soldiers pierced His side with a spear, and immediately there came out blood and water" *(John 19:34)*. What does the blood represent? Remember in the Old Testament how the sacrifice had to be slain and its blood sprinkled on the mercy seat for the forgiveness of the people's sin? The innocent blood of Jesus was shed on the cross at Calvary for forgiveness of your sins. As you partake of the Lord's Supper, it is a means of grace by which you can celebrate what Jesus has done for you. The bread symbolizes the brokenness Jesus experienced. The juice/wine is symbolic of the blood poured out to cleanse you of your sin.

What does the water represent?

_____

_____

I believe the water represents water baptism. "Or do you not know that all of us who have been baptized into Christ Jesus have been baptized into His death? Therefore, we have been buried with Him through baptism into death, in order that as Christ was raised from the dead through the glory of the Father, so we too might walk in newness of life" *(Rom. 6:3-4)*.

After you accept Jesus into your heart, you should follow through with water baptism. Water baptism is an outward expression that symbolizes you have been baptized into Christ's death, so you are dead to sin and alive to walk in newness of life in Jesus Christ!

Throughout your life, brokenness and separation from God occurs because of sin. When you accept Jesus Christ as your Savior, His blood, shed on the cross, restores your relationship with God when you seek His forgiveness. Remember, Jesus has experienced the separation from God, so you do not have to. You have the Lord's Supper and water baptism, which are two forms of a means of grace, that God imparts to every believer. The next time you can participate in the Lord's Supper, allow it to bring forth newness into your life. A new life is what Jesus intended for you as he hung on the cross at Calvary.

If you are unsure of your salvation, please pray the following prayer out loud:

Jesus,

I've finally come to the end of my rope. I realize I am a sinner and I need you. Jesus, please forgive me of all my sins and please come live in my heart. Please heal my heart and help me to give You glory in all that I do. In the name of Jesus, Amen.

If you just asked Jesus into your heart, I would like to be the first to welcome you into the Kingdom of God. Bless you! Angels are rejoicing! Please be sure to follow through with water baptism. I'm so excited for you, Beloved!

PRAYER TIME

Holy Lord, thank you for the gift of salvation. Thank you for sending me Your Son, Jesus, to be my scapegoat and take away all my sins. Wow! Your love for me is beyond comprehension. I can't even begin to fathom how much You love me, yet You do. Thank you for giving me wisdom and discernment about the things that go on in the heavenly realm. Help me to see how important I am to You and how nothing can separate me from Your love. I want to experience the agape love from You in a mighty way and show this love to others, so they might see Christ in me. Lord, thank you for opening doors for me to get involved in Bible studies with others who have similar interests as I do. Thank you for surrounding me with good Christian friends and family, so we can encourage each other to be the best people we can be, so we can be there for each other in the tough times and be there for the joyous times. Thank you for loving me! In the name of Jesus, Amen.

Epilogue

"And this I pray, that your love may abound still more and more in real knowledge and all discernment, so that you may approve the things that are excellent, in order to be sincere and blameless until the day of Christ; having been filled with the fruit of righteousness which comes through Jesus Christ, to the glory and praise of God." *Philippians 1:9-11*

Beloved, this is my prayer for you as you walk forward in your new life. I hope that you can use what you have learned and apply it to your life in the coming weeks, months, and years.

There will still be trials and testing in your life. You can be victorious as you and God face the battles of life together.

I have enjoyed going on this journey with you. Thank you for allowing me to be a small part of your life. I hope that you will look at events in your life and say, "It Matters!"

About the Author

Amy Lynne grew up in the suburbs of Birmingham, Alabama, and still lives in the area today. She has shared her testimony in the book *Behind the Mask*. She desires to help refresh people spiritually, and she desires to impart hope and healing to people who are frustrated with life.

Amy has a daughter, son-in-law, and two grandchildren. She lives on the lake and enjoys having friends and family over for boat rides and fun in the sun in the spring and summer. She is a member of a local Baptist church and is involved in teaching the Word with other women and young GA (Girls in Action) girls.

One day, she might get around to getting married again if God choses to bring "the one" into her life.

Morgan James
Speakers Group

We connect Morgan James published authors with live and online events and audiences whom will benefit from their expertise.

Morgan James makes all of our titles available through the Library for All Charity Organization.

www.LibraryForAll.org

9 781683 505990